David R. Cerbone is Professor of Philosophy at West Virginia University, where he teaches a regularly oversubscribed course on existentialism for undergraduates. He is the author of two books, *Understanding Phenomenology* (2006) and *Heidegger: A Guide for the Perplexed* (2008), and more than 30 articles and reviews on Heidegger and Wittgenstein, as well as the phenomenological and existentialist traditions more generally. He currently serves as one of the editors for the *Routledge Research in Phenomenology* series.

David lives with his wife and three children (along with two dogs, three cats, a rabbit and a guinea pig) in rural West Virginia. In addition to philosophy, his other passion is photography. His work can be seen at several galleries in West Virginia.

EXISTENTIALISM
ALL THAT MATTERS

EXISTENTIALISM

David R. Cerbone

ALL THAT MATTERS

First published in Great Britain in 2015 by Hodder and Stoughton. An Hachette UK company.

This edition published in 2015 by John Murray Learning

Paperback ISBN 9781473601437

eBook ISBN 9781473601451

10 9 8 7 6 5 4 3 2 1

Typeset by Cenveo® Publisher Services.

Printed and bound in Great Britain by CPI Group (UK) Ltd., Croydon, CR0 4YY.

John Murray Learning policy is to use papers that are natural, renewable and recyclable products and made from wood grown in sustainable forests. The logging and manufacturing processes are expected to conform to the environmental regulations of the country of origin.

Hodder & Stoughton Ltd
Carmelite House
50 Victoria Embankment
London EC4Y 0DZ
www.hodder.co.uk

For the many students of Philosophy 355 (and Philosophy 121 before that) at WVU, who have over the years worked with me to discover what really matters in existentialism.

Contents

Prologue

Before his death, Rabbi Zusya said 'In the coming world, they will not ask me: "Why were you not Moses?" They will ask me: "Why were you not Zusya?"'

The parable of Rabbi Zusya's judgment comes from the Hasidic tradition in Judaism. Rabbi Zusya of Hanipol was a Hasidic master or *zaddik*, and, as with other such masters, there are many legends and parables associated with him. The parable is recounted by Martin Buber in the first volume of his *Tales of the Hasidim*. In the *Tales*, the parable is entitled 'The Query of Queries', which gives some indication of its significance. Buber is an important 20th-century philosopher within Judaism, but his interests and significance extend beyond the Jewish tradition. His most famous work, *I and Thou*, is often ranked among works in the existentialist tradition, and so in citing this parable at the outset of this book, I am not roaming as far afield as it might appear.

There is something both familiar and paradoxical about Zusya's question. We are all conversant with expressions such as 'Just be yourself', 'That's not who I really am', 'I was not myself yesterday', and so on, but if we try to dig down beneath these familiar expressions and statements, they become increasingly puzzling. After all, if Zusya is Zusya, how could he be, or even have been, anything else? We can readily understand how Zusya might have failed to do some particular thing or reach some particular goal. We can also readily understand how he might have failed to be more like someone else. But how could he have failed to be himself?

In *The Ethics of Ambiguity*, the existentialist philosopher and writer Simone de Beauvoir asserts that 'in the very condition of man there enters the possibility of not fulfilling this condition'.[1] This seems to accord with the reproach Zusya imagines awaiting him 'in the coming world'. To fail to be Zusya is for Zusya to have failed to 'fulfil' his condition. But what does that mean? Consider an acorn. An acorn has a very specific condition, which includes a very specific form of fulfilment: an acorn fulfils its condition by growing into a mighty oak. But as even a casual walk through the woods will reveal, most acorns do not grow into oak trees. Many – if not most – of the acorns strewn under and around their parent oak trees will be eaten by animals, wither or rot away, be crunched underfoot by hikers, and so on. So it would seem that in the 'very condition' of acorns there lies the possibility of not fulfilling this condition. But if this is so, de Beauvoir's assertion becomes more puzzling in that it no longer appears to be marking out something about the human condition in particular or in contrast to the condition of other kinds of things.

To see that there might be something distinctive about the human condition in contrast to that of the acorn, notice first that the 'query of queries' is not something acorns themselves ever ask. Though I might stand before the acorn lying fallow and ask, 'Why are you not a mighty oak?', it would be foolish to expect an answer. That Zusya raises the question about being Zusya for himself suggests that the issue of accountability or answerability arises for Zusya and the rest of us: we, unlike the acorn, have to answer for who we are or who we become. The question matters – or can matter – to us in a way that it doesn't for something like an acorn.

In the Introduction to the *Tales*, Buber contrasts 'the ideal pattern of the individual limned by the Creator, and what he actually is'. When Zusya worries about the coming world, he is worried about how he'll 'measure up' to that ideal pattern. Further questions arise here: what is that 'ideal pattern' and how is Zusya supposed to know what it is? That these questions arise here mark another difference between a human being and an acorn. It is pretty easy to say what an acorn is supposed to become: the ideal pattern for an acorn is growing into a mighty oak. The measure for acorns is thus readily available. But what is that measure when it comes to being human? What is it that any of us is supposed to be? Talk about an ideal pattern suggests an answer laid up somewhere, awaiting us in the 'coming world' perhaps, but if it is that hidden, we can only feel anxious about it while we are living out our lives here and now. Acorns are not anxious about becoming oaks or not. They just fall to the ground and then either grow or do not.

The question of who we are supposed to be haunts us in a way that it doesn't for an acorn. It is a question for us to ponder, for us to ask of ourselves, but it is also an importantly different question. For us, the question is personal, whereas the question raised about the acorn is generic. Whatever the ideal pattern is for an acorn, it is one that pertains to all acorns in the same way: an acorn is supposed to become an oak tree, full stop. But Zusya worries that he will have failed to be Zusya, not just a full or complete human being (whatever that might be). In this way, the parable brings into view the particular kind of project that I see at the heart of existentialism: the project of becoming an individual. Søren Kierkegaard, a founding figure of existentialism, writes in the preface to *The Sickness Unto Death* of a kind of 'Christian heroism' that involves 'risk[ing] unreservedly being oneself, an individual human being, this specific individual human being alone before God, alone in this enormous exertion and enormous accountability'[2]. The Christian hero feels a similar accountability – and a similar risk of failure – as Hasidism's Zusya. The question Kierkegaard's remark raises, just as much as the parable of Zusya does, is one of how we are to understand this talk of 'enormous exertion'. What exactly is difficult, what stands in the way of being 'this specific individual human being'? Aren't we – each of us – that already? What more do I have to do in order to be an individual beyond just being this person, numerically distinct from all others?

These sorts of questions will inform our exploration of the existentialist tradition in 19th- and 20th-century philosophy, as each of the figures considered – Kierkegaard, Friedrich Nietzsche, Martin Heidegger, Jean-Paul Sartre, Albert Camus and Simone de Beauvoir – offer related, though distinct, conceptions of the task of becoming an individual. In many ways, existentialism's concern with this task is no different from many earlier philosophical points of view. Existentialism is not discontinuous with the philosophical tradition out of which it emerges. At the same time, part of what is exciting about studying existentialism is the way it is also a radical critique of, and departure from, that prior tradition. Indeed, for existentialism, part of what stands in the way of our becoming individuals is our being bogged down with traditional assumptions and ideas (that there is an ideal pattern out there that we just need to figure out or discover might be one of them). We need to break free of tradition while at the same time preserving and transforming many of its core concerns. I will next sketch out in very distilled form a key existentialist insight or perspective in relation to these traditional assumptions and ideas. Making this kind of shift in perspective will give us the right point of view for appreciating the novelty of existentialism's concern with the possibility of each of us becoming 'this specific individual human being', nothing more, but also nothing less.

1

The existentialist insight

... man materializes in the world, encounters himself, and only afterward defines himself.

Sartre, Existentialism is a Humanism

As movements or schools of thought in philosophy go, existentialism is a peculiar one. Some sense of why this is so can be gained just by thinking about the origins of the label. The term 'existentialism' (actually the French *l'existentialisme*) was first coined by the philosopher and playwright Gabriel Marcel in the early 1940s. Marcel came up with the term to apply to the thought of his friends Jean-Paul Sartre and Simone de Beauvoir. Marcel did not pull the term out of thin air: there was precedent for the label in the German philosopher Karl Jaspers' idea of *Existenzphilosophie*, as well as Martin Heidegger's idea that when it comes to the kind of beings we are, our *essence* lies in our *existence*. There are also deeper roots for the term, as we will see in later chapters. In any event, Sartre at first resisted the label, claiming not to know what it meant. But the label stuck and Sartre discovered that his thinking was being described as 'existentialism' in various Parisian intellectual circles and that all manner of connotations were accruing to the term. Better, then, to own the term and thereby gain some control over its meaning, and so by 1945 Sartre was describing himself as an existentialist thinker.

Once the term was coined, it exhibited a remarkable backward spread, and therein lies its peculiarity. It turned out that there had been existentialists for quite a long time, even though none of them would have identified themselves in such terms. The label stuck most directly to those thinkers, Heidegger and Jaspers, whose ideas and terminology had served as inspiration for the term, although for his part, Heidegger, who lived until 1976, vehemently protested its applicability. Other

French contemporaries of Sartre and de Beauvoir, such as Maurice Merleau-Ponty and Albert Camus, came to be associated with the label, as well as the Spanish philosopher, Ortega y Gasset. But the term managed to reach back even further, into the 19th century, to the German philosopher Friedrich Nietzsche and the Danish thinker Søren Kierkegaard, who comes closest perhaps to being a founding figure in the 'movement'. The label also managed to reach beyond thinkers typically identified as philosophers. The Russian novelist Fyodor Dostoyevsky, whose *Notes from Underground* paints perhaps the most abject portrait of the lone individual, is often included in the ranks of existentialist thinkers. But still earlier thinkers came to be identified with existentialist thinking, albeit in ever looser ways: Shakespeare, Pascal and even the medieval philosopher St Augustine show certain existentialist proclivities. One might liken Marcel's coinage to a rock being thrown into a pond: the rock's impact creates a series of concentric waves that grow continually weaker as they travel further from its point of entry.

No set of philosophical ideas emerges in a vacuum, but always draws upon and engages with previous ones. Existentialism is no exception. Indeed, as a relatively late entry in the western philosophical tradition, it is all but impossible not to find precedents for, and lines of influence leading to, its central ideas. After all, none other than Socrates showed a deep concern with the self and self-knowledge, which indicates that the roots of existentialism run very deep, all the way back to nearly the beginning of western philosophy. But the advent of *modern* philosophy sets the stage for existentialist ideas in a more vivid and urgent way. The challenges modern philosophy confronts were largely absent from earlier stages of the tradition. I cannot document here these challenges and their importance for existentialism in their entirety, but I will indicate a couple of directions.

Very broadly speaking, the emergence of modern philosophy is prompted by the rise of modern science with the Scientific Revolution of the 16th and 17th centuries and by if not the decline, at least the fragmentation of religious thinking, due most notably to the Protestant Reformation of the 16th century. Taken together, these various ideas create a crisis of authority. Luther challenged the traditional authority of the Church, whose teachings until that time had been literally sacrosanct. By questioning the hierarchical power structure of the Church, a structure that culminated in the supreme authority of the Pope, Luther placed a new emphasis on the individual believer: what mattered for religious faith was not the acceptance of doctrines and practices dictated by church officials, but instead the individual's own conscience, which could stand in an unmediated relationship with God. (In some writings, Luther goes so far as to say that no outward acts have any bearing on one's status as a Christian.) Each and every Christian, according to Luther, has to work out his or her own relationship to God for him- or herself.

The new sciences – the physics of Galileo and Newton, the astronomy of Copernicus and Kepler – also posed threats for traditional religious ideas. The world-view of Christianity depicted the cosmos as ordered in accord with, and so reflecting, God's will and beneficence. The heavens comprised perfect spherical objects – heavenly bodies in both senses of the term – all of which revolved around the Earth, which stood at the centre of God's creation. And that was as it should be, since God had created human beings in His own image. Where else would such beings reside in the grand scheme of things but at the very centre? That picture was pretty much shattered by the new sciences: using the newly invented telescope, Galileo showed that the Moon was a mountainous, pockmarked body, a far cry from the perfectly smooth, perfectly spherical object one would have expected. And with the Copernican revolution, astronomy displaced the Earth from its central position; it became one more planet among others, orbiting one more star among others. With these developments, the question of humanity's place in the universe took on a much starker tone, as the ready-made answer no longer had the kind of easy availability it once had. If God did have a plan for us, that was going to be much more difficult to figure out.

These developments in astronomy, along with the rise of mechanistic physics, disrupted a picture of reality as filled with meaning. The new physics banished older ideas of purposes and goals – Aristotle's notion of a 'final cause' that had been embraced by Catholic teaching – in explaining how and why things move. As a result, the whole category of *value* undergoes a crisis: where in the world are values to be found? Indeed, are they found there at all? By prompting such questions, these modern developments have the effect of throwing us back upon ourselves, to figure out exactly who we are such that we can make sense of notions like *meaning*, *purpose* and *value*. Hence we see with the rise of modern philosophy a new emphasis on **subjectivity**. Descartes' famous *Cogito, ergo sum* ('I think, therefore I am') marks the beginning of modern philosophy, while Kant declared that the motto of the Enlightenment is *Sapere aude!* ('Dare to be wise!'), which Kant glosses as, 'Have courage to use your *own* understanding!'

The distinctively modern picture of human beings as cast into a meaningless world without any preordained aim or purpose forms the backdrop to existentialism. While some strands of modern philosophy strive to resist this kind of picture (to be a modern philosopher only requires confronting the challenges raised by the new sciences and the new religious landscape, rather than endorsing any one way of meeting them), existentialism by and large embraces such a picture and, in many ways, radicalizes it. What I mean here is this: for existentialism, the lesson of modernity is that the world has nothing to offer in terms of determining or validating any way we might try to understand ourselves and our place in the world. No story about who we are or why we are here can ever be shown to be the 'right' story. The conclusion the existentialist draws is that *there is no deep truth about the kind of beings we are*. But – and here comes the radicalizing move – that conclusion is *the* deep truth about who we are: we are beings for whom there is no fact of the matter about who we are. We are beings who strive to understand ourselves and our place in the world without there being any way of validating that self-understanding by appealing to how

▲ Patrick Stewart (Vladimir) and Ian McKellen (Estragon) in a 2009 production of Samuel Beckett's *Waiting for Godot* at the Theatre Royal, London.

the world is. Sometimes this idea is summarized by saying that we are *self-interpreting* beings.

Now the big question is what one does with this existentialist insight. Broadly speaking, we might see existentialism as asking what else must be true about the kind of beings we are if we are indeed self-interpreting beings? It turns out, according to existentialism, that many other things must be true. In particular, existentialism emphasizes our **freedom**: in order to be self-interpreting beings, we must be beings who are fundamentally free. We are, in Sartre's famous words, 'condemned to be free'. With this freedom comes the possibility of **anxiety**, **anguish** and **despair**. We will consider these notions at length elsewhere.

We can also ask what follows from the idea that we are self-interpreting beings. In particular, we might wonder if this idea somehow selects among the various possible self-interpretations human beings might construct for themselves. If it is true that the deep truth about us is that there is no deep truth – or if it is true that we are just self-interpreting beings – then what kind of self-interpretation should we construct? We should bear in mind here that constructing a self-interpretation is not an abstract, intellectual exercise, but a matter of living out a life with a particular shape and direction. So in effect existentialism is asking the age-old question of how we should live, but with the twist that this question is posed with the realization that the world will offer nothing to help with an answer.

It is quite natural to think that this movement beyond existentialism's core idea is rather hopeless. Why think that there is *any* preferred or superior self-interpretation if there is no deep truth about the kind of beings we are beyond being self-interpreting beings? Why not just say that 'anything goes'? Or, perhaps, that 'nothing goes'? It may seem that we are stuck with either a rampant relativism or an especially bleak kind of **nihilism** once we have been brought around to the existentialist point of view. And, indeed, existentialism is often associated with such despondency. The literature of Samuel Beckett, which typically depicts human beings as mired in a futile longing for purpose and meaning – waiting for a Godot who never comes – is one example of this distinctively existentialist form of despair. The stories and novels of Franz Kafka offer another example. But while there are certain wings or factions of existentialism that counsel this form of despair, I do not think such a view should be taken as the last word on the matter. On the contrary, I see the main figures associated with existentialism (with the exception of Camus perhaps, but that is a question we will wrestle with in Chapter 6) as insisting that its core idea need not entail a chaotic relativism or despairing nihilism. What existentialism endeavours to show is that there are better, more **authentic** ways of responding to, or continuing on from, the key insight that we are nothing but self-interpreting beings, since there are ways of living that do a better (and worse) job of reflecting or incorporating just that idea. The details of how existentialism might develop and defend this claim will concern us throughout this book.

2

Kierkegaard: selfhood and despair

That the knowing spirit is an existing individual spirit, and that every human being is such an entity existing for himself, is a truth I cannot too often repeat.

Kierkegaard, Concluding Unscientific Postscript

▶ Truth is subjectivity

In Chapter 1, I noted that one source of existentialist thinking is modern philosophy's more general concern with the notion of subjectivity. Modern philosophy begins with Descartes' *Cogito, ergo sum*, the discovery of the self as the basis for all knowledge, including scientific knowledge and knowledge of God. I also noted in Chapter 1 that existentialism can often be understood as radicalizing insights and ideas that pervade modern philosophy more generally. This preoccupation with subjectivity is a case in point. Kierkegaard is famous for announcing that 'truth is subjectivity'. Kierkegaard is suggesting here that what really matters is to be found at the level of, and within, the ongoing life of the existing individual. That Kierkegaard gives pride of place to the existing individual and devotes considerable attention to articulating its special character is why he is viewed as something of a founding figure in existentialist thought.

Kierkegaard's championing of subjectivity begins with a thoroughgoing (and generally negative) appraisal of objectivity as an overarching ideal for all thinking. 'The way of objective reflection makes the subject accidental, and thereby transforms existence into something indifferent, something vanishing.'[3] Inscribed into the *telos* of objectivity is a kind of effacement of the very subject who aspires to be objective: 'The existing subject proposes *qua* thinker to abstract from the fact that he is occupied in existing, in order to be *sub specie aeterni*.'[4] To get a feel for what Kierkegaard is driving at here, consider a more recent turn of phrase that does much the same duty as the terminology employed in Kierkegaard's remark: rather than thinking *sub specie aeterni*, we might think of the aspiration to full or complete objectivity as the desire to take up what Thomas Nagel has dubbed a 'view from nowhere'. Although there is a sense in which such a view might take in one's own existence, as that is one of the many objective facts of the world to be duly noted, it does so *only* as an objective fact, something taken in from the outside, so to speak. Fundamentally and essentially absent from this view is any kind of 'inside' perspective, any sense of 'inhabiting' the view. There is something doubly problematic about this talk of inhabitation when it comes to the view from nowhere: first, anyone who might aspire to take up such a view is always, as an 'existing individual', precisely *somewhere* and so never really manages the feat (a God's-eye point of view requires that one be a god). As Kierkegaard notes: 'If an existing individual were really able to transcend himself, the truth would be for him something final and complete; but where is the point at which he is outside himself?'[5] Second, even if one could manage it, one's taking up or occupying such a view is irrelevant in terms of the 'content' of the view. Indeed, that is just the point about objectivity: if something is objectively true, then it does not matter who it is who believes it; it does not matter if it is believed at all. If *p* is true, then it is just as well that I believe or assert it as someone else, and should we all cease to believe or assert it, the truth of *p* would remain just the same. The truth of *p* has, we might say, nothing to do with me, even if I happen to be the one who first discovered or asserted it.

▲ Søren Kierkegaard (1813–55).

The aspiration to objectivity is often connected with the notion of *disinterestedness*. Insofar as I bring interests, preferences or desires to the inquiry, I thereby diminish its objectivity. Although I think Kierkegaard detects problems with the ideal of objectivity in terms of an existing individual actually ever fully attaining it (because, again, one always takes up and works through a view from somewhere in particular), he also recognizes that there are domains where aspiring to this sort of disinterestedness is perfectly in order. That is, in some contexts we do certainly want people to try to factor out their own idiosyncratic feelings, preferences and desires when trying to determine what is so. When scientists test hypotheses, design experiments, analyse data etc., we do not expect or want them to rely overly on how they feel about the data, nor would it be proper for their inquiry to be guided overly by what they want the result to be.

So the notion of objectivity in and of itself is not the problem. Kierkegaard is not a sceptic or relativist in the usual senses of these terms, even if he has misgivings about the possibility of anyone ever being fully or completely objective (anyone with a conception of human beings as fallible would likely agree on this point). Kierkegaard's problem with objectivity concerns its applicability in a very specific domain, namely an individual's own ongoing existence. Consider again Kierkegaard's remark in the *Postscript*: 'The way of objective reflection makes the subject accidental, and thereby transforms existence into something indifferent, something vanishing.'[6] Such a transformation is precisely what makes objective reflection inappropriate in this domain: if what is at issue is my own existence, then my standing as a subject is far from 'accidental', nor is it 'something indifferent' with respect to the matter at hand (as my subjectivity *is* the matter at hand). There is something distinctively perverse, Kierkegaard thinks, in striving to reflect on oneself in as detached a manner as possible, as it requires factoring out what is most vital to one's deliberations: 'While objective thought is indifferent to the thinking subject and his existence, the subjective thinker is an existing individual essentially interested in his own thinking, existing as he does in his thought.'[7] To be 'essentially interested' precludes the kind of disinterestedness required by objectivity: if I factor out my own interests and preferences, then I have omitted from consideration precisely what constitutes my concern, namely me.

Someone may object that Kierkegaard's elimination of the possibility of taking up an objective stance toward oneself – one's own subjectivity – is a bit too neat. After all, we sometimes do try to view ourselves in a detached manner; we try to get clear about ourselves, evaluate our feelings, preferences and actions as though from the outside. We weigh our reasons for our decisions not just in terms of the intensity of our feelings, but in terms of the aptness of those reasons, so that we may justify our choices and decisions not just to ourselves but also to others. Moreover, our choices and decisions are not made in a vacuum, independently of how things are in the world, and so we both want and need to have a sense of 'what is so' in charting our courses of action. A certain degree of objectivity, of what the ideal of objectivity aspires to, would seem to be not just desirable but even essential.

It is not at all clear to me that Kierkegaard would resist this line of reasoning. But at the same time, he maintains that this way of thinking has limits. Reflection on one's own life – on what matters most – requires not cool detachment but passion. Moreover, all such reflection necessarily confronts *objective uncertainty*. Even if there is a 'right answer' to the question of what matters most to me – of what is most worthy of my devotion – the rightness of such an answer is not something I or anyone else can know here and now. But my ongoing existence is precisely that – ongoing – and so I must commit myself without the luxury of having the answers at hand. Were I to wait for such answers, then my life would take on that shape – one of cautiously waiting, weighing evidence about this or that option, testing out this or that possibility. And that would be the sum of my life. Am I better off that way?

Here we see the problem with aspiring to objectivity in this domain: given the objective uncertainty each of us confronts, the correctness of choosing to strive for greater objectivity is itself objectively uncertain. There is, we might say, no objective justification for striving to determine the shape of one's life in as objective a manner as possible. Indeed, striving in this manner may mean missing out on something far more meaningful and satisfying. No one can say in advance, but we confront our own lives here and now. One's own life as one's own is an *absolute singularity*: it is the one and only life to be had and it unfolds in time in an irreversible, unrepeatable manner. There are thus significant limits to the applicability of the ideal of objectivity: I cannot gather evidence, test various hypotheses, run various experiments, and then apply all of that in order to make a decision *now*. Doing all those things would have taken up a more or less significant stretch of my life, which cannot now be repeated or lived differently.

We can now, I think, see a little more clearly what Kierkegaard means by declaring that 'truth is subjectivity'. He is *not* saying that all truth is subjective, relative, or some such thing. Again, he is not denying the idea of objectivity in general. We might read him here as saying that the truth about existence is subjectivity, that there is no escaping the particularity of one's individual existence. As he recognizes, there is something distinctly trivial-sounding about this assertion, as it is not exactly information or news to anyone: 'To be sure, every human being is a bit of a subject, in a sense. But now to strive to become what one already is: who would take the pains to waste his time on such a task, involving the greatest imaginable degree of resignation?'[8] But precisely because it sounds so trivial, involving as it does becoming what one already is, 'it is commonly assumed that no art or skill is required in order to be subjective'[9].

▶ Structures of the self

Consider again Kierkegaard's claims that 'every human is a bit of a subject, in a sense' and that 'it is commonly assumed that no art or skill is required in order to be subjective'. Why is every human only 'a bit of a subject' (and only 'in a sense') and what is wrong with the common assumption he derides? We might answer this question by attending to another work, *The Sickness Unto Death*, which offers a conception of the self that lays bare the difficulties involved in becoming one. The work opens with the following almost wilfully obscure passage:

> *The human being is spirit. But what is spirit? Spirit is the self. But what is the self? The self is a relation which relates to itself, or that in the relation which is its relating to itself. The self is not the relation but the relation's relating to itself.*[10]

Difficult as this may sound, Kierkegaard's talk here of the self as involving 'a relation' provides a way for thinking about becoming a self as an achievement, and so as something one can fail to be. One is not a self just by being numerically distinct from everyone else if the kind of relation in question fails to obtain. Kierkegaard in this work calls the various forms this failure can take **despair**. Schematically put, in despair I fail to be a self by failing to be 'a relation which relates to itself'. To fill this in a bit, let us examine how the opening passage continues:

> A human being is a synthesis of the infinite and the finite, of the temporal and the eternal, of freedom and necessity.[11]

The trio of pairs Kierkegaard offers here gives us a kind of foothold for understanding his opening appeal to the notion of a relation: becoming a self involves establishing, and maintaining, a relation between the paired factors indicated here. Despair, by contrast, 'is the imbalance in a relation of synthesis, in a relation which relates to itself'[12].

To get a feel for what Kierkegaard means by imbalance here, consider the last pair: freedom and necessity. How does human existence involve these two factors and how can I experience an imbalance between them? To start with the first question: we experience ourselves in terms of necessity in the sense that there are aspects of ourselves over which we have little or no control. The basic contours of our bodies – that I have this body and not another one – is one example of necessity, but we might also think of the basic contours of our temperament and attitudes, our likes and dislikes, and so on. My past provides another example, since what I have done and what has happened to me are not things that I can now undo. At the same time, we also experience ourselves in terms of there being *open possibilities*, in the sense that things lie ahead of us and these may be very different than how they are now. We can change things that we don't like about ourselves, for example, or change the ways in which we live. Such changes are not easy most of the time – it is not a matter of just deciding to be different – but the main thing is that such differences show up as possible at all. Such open possibilities are indications of our freedom. But how might these two factors become imbalanced?

One way these factors may fail to be aligned is when I feel 'stuck' in my life as I am leading it. In such circumstances, I feel overwhelmed by necessity, by the feeling that there is no other way things *can* be. Here my freedom has been eclipsed; I no longer see other possibilities beyond the way things are. But the imbalance can go the other way as well: rather than feeling stuck, I may instead feel adrift amidst an endless series of possibilities cut free from any facts about who I am or have been. If I spend my time idly indulging in fantasies involving more heroic or accomplished or just happier versions of myself, but without actually doing anything to realize them, then I am in despair just as much as when I feel hopelessly tied to the circumstances in which I find myself. In either case, I am closing myself off to an aspect of my own existence. Kierkegaard calls the kind of despair marked by being adrift among unrealized possibilities *weakness*, since I long for some other way to be while feeling unable to attain it; alternatively, the feeling of being stuck can devolve into what he calls **defiance**, where I reject the idea of possibilities altogether and wallow instead in how I actually am.

The possibility – and indeed the prevalence – of despair is a mark of the human condition. 'The possibility of this sickness is man's advantage over the beast'[13], since for animals there is no issue of a balance or imbalance between two factors. The beast is in a very real sense just where it is, with no awareness of a past behind it or a future lying ahead of it. Despair is an advantage, since only a being capable of despair can become a self. Overcoming despair is a necessary condition of becoming a self. But how does one do that? Kierkegaard emphatically rejects what we might call a 'go it alone' strategy, whereby I struggle on my own to eradicate my feelings of despair. That such efforts are futile and serve only to intensify my despair can be discerned in the other two pairs of factors in addition to freedom and necessity, which involve the infinite and the eternal. Establishing and maintaining a relation to those are not something I can hope to do all by myself. To think otherwise is to indulge a fantasy of control that is itself a form of despair. Hence the 'formula' Kierkegaard gives in *The Sickness Unto Death*:

> *This then is the formula which describes the state of the self when despair is completely eradicated: in relating to itself and wanting to be itself, the self is grounded transparently in the power that established it.*[14]

▲ Kierkegaard's grave in Assistens Cemetery, Copenhagen.

Recall the objective uncertainty one confronts in becoming subjective. By turning 'inward' I confront the issue of commitment: I have to choose what shape to give my life as it continues and those choices matter in that there is no undoing their effects. Moreover, I cannot now know what effects those choices will really have and so I must choose under conditions of ignorance. If I am wishy-washy and dither – evading the issue of choice – then I am committing myself to a dithering life and this too is a form of despair. Alternatively, I can go 'all in', staking myself decisively to something (or someone – marriage is a good example of the kind of commitment at issue). But doing this requires *faith*, since the 'success' of those decisions depends on factors well beyond anything I can control or make happen. That is why Kierkegaard says that 'faith is precisely the contradiction between the infinite passion of the individual's inwardness and the objective uncertainty'[15]. Faith is a kind of willingness to let things matter while acknowledging one's inability to eliminate that uncertainty. To be a self – fully and without despair – is to be what Kierkegaard calls a **knight of faith**. Such a knight embraces the 'contradiction' between 'infinite passion' and 'objective uncertainty', thereby putting his or her trust in **God** rather than chasing a fantasy of total control or succumbing to despair. Through faith I become an individual by letting something count for me absolutely or unconditionally. Doing so requires 'focus'. Someone lacking such focus has a soul that 'is disintegrated from the start'[16]. That person 'will be forever running errands in life, never enter the eternal; for at the very moment he is almost there he will suddenly discover that he has forgotten something and so must go back.'[17]

Kierkegaard's image of the person 'forever running errands in life' is one of someone constantly busy, but also perpetually scattered. Although being busy in this way serves to fill up one's days – indeed, time often seems to race by – living this way involves none of the passionate inwardness Kierkegaard thinks becoming an individual requires. To be consumed by 'errands' is to lack faith in anything ultimate; if I am just busy being busy, then there is nothing really that my life is all about. I may feel like I always have something to do and somewhere to be, but all of this scurrying about does not add up to anything or make a unified whole. Whether I feel it particularly or not, in leading such a life I am mired in despair. As we will see, later existentialist thinkers – especially Heidegger – are also centrally concerned with this notion of the busy but nonetheless complacent life absorbed in everyday mundane tasks, as well as with the possibility (and promise) of such a life's being disrupted or even shattered.

3

Nietzsche and the task of self-creation

God is dead. God remains dead.
And we have killed him.

Nietzsche, The Gay Science

▶ Perspectivism and the death of God

On the face of it, Kierkegaard and Nietzsche would appear to have little in common. Kierkegaard emphasizes repeatedly the importance of God and one's duty to Him, whereas Nietzsche is famous for declaring that '**God is dead**'. Nietzsche would thus appear to be diametrically opposed to Kierkegaard. Things are not always as they seem, however, as the nature of Kierkegaard's commitment to Christianity indicates greater proximity to Nietzsche than one might think. In particular, we need to keep in mind Kierkegaard's championing of subjectivity – of the task of 'becoming subjective' – and so his critique of the ideal of objectivity. While that notion is viewed with some suspicion in Kierkegaard's philosophy, especially when it comes to questions of ultimate concern, Nietzsche's animus toward it is far more thoroughgoing. Indeed, the very idea pulls itself apart: a view – or, in Nietzsche's favoured term, a 'perspective' – is always *located*, and so always in some way conditioned by that location and by the particularities of the creature so located. Nietzsche's **perspectivism** is founded on the recognition that all views are indeed points of view, i.e. all views are located and so conditioned by that fact. All views, in other words, are interpretations. To acknowledge this is, for Nietzsche, just what it means to acknowledge the death of God.

But the idea that all views are interpretations raises the further question of the status of perspectivism. Simply put, if all views are interpretations, as perspectivism

▲ Friedrich Nietzsche (1844–1900).

maintains, doesn't that claim apply to perspectivism itself, and doesn't that mean that perspectivism too is only an interpretation? I think it is clear that Nietzsche would have to answer the last question in the affirmative. To do otherwise would court self-refutation, i.e. it would be patently inconsistent of Nietzsche to declare that all views are interpretations while conferring on that very declaration some superior status (an announcement *sub specie aeternitas*). Indeed, Nietzsche seems eager to apply this inference to his own declarations: 'Granted this too is only interpretation – and you will be eager enough to raise this objection? – well, so much the better.'[18]

That perspectivism is itself an interpretation does not mean that Nietzsche refrains from according to it some superiority over other views. One 'virtue' of perspectivism is precisely its willingness to acknowledge its own status as an interpretation, which other points of view have largely been unwilling to do. That is, other views aspire to be, and present themselves as being, something more than interpretations, something along the lines of absolutely correct and universally binding doctrines. The history of philosophy abounds with examples of such claims of having found the one right view (and for Nietzsche, the histories of religion and morality have followed a parallel trajectory). That there have been so many examples – so many views vying for the crown of objectivity – suggests the folly of the enterprise for Nietzsche: 'There is no denying that *in the long run* every one of these great teachers of a purpose was vanquished by laughter, reason and nature.'[19]

The sheer diversity of views indicates that some factors are operative in the formation of these views other than the implausible notion that some one or more of these thinkers has really achieved some apprehension of the unvarnished truth. At work in the development and championing of these various views are precisely the kinds of interests and needs that Nietzsche thinks are at work in the formation of all views, his own included. 'For assuming that one is a person, one necessarily also has the philosophy that belongs to that person.'[20] Rather than a disinterested taking in or recording of how things are, every philosophical point of view is a reflection and projection of the person whose view it is: show me your philosophical commitments and I'll tell you the kind of person you are (and vice versa). But philosophers and other thinkers have generally managed to hide this fact, from their audience and even from themselves. Philosophy has been an 'unconscious disguise of physiological needs ... and a *misunderstanding of the body*'.[21] Since previous philosophical views have hidden or denied their origins and so their status as interpretations conditioned by the needs and interests of the ones doing the interpreting, Nietzsche can thereby claim for his own perspective a kind of honesty and consistency lacking in most others.

For Nietzsche, what explains these perspectives is not (or at least not primarily) their latching on to reality as being absolutely the way the perspectives in question claim it to be, but the ways in which these perspectives have been both consciously and unconsciously motivated by the needs and interests of those whose perspectives they are. The increasing availability of such explanations is for Nietzsche precisely what gives the lie to what he calls 'metaphysical explanations', which seek to confer an absolute status on what is really only one perspective among others. The ironic twist in Nietzsche's account of the demise of metaphysics is that it is undone by its own commitments. Metaphysics is informed by the demand for truth, for getting completely clear about how things are irrespective of the consequences (what Nietzsche refers to as 'truth at any price'). But striving to satisfy that desire gives rise to increasingly sophisticated scientific accounts of reality, and these accounts reveal the ways in which a point of view – a conception of the world – is conditioned by a variety of psychological and physiological factors. Such a revelation undermines the very metaphysical commitments that prompted the discovery of these factors. The desire to acquire knowledge, which has been fuelled by metaphysics, leads to its downfall: as we learn more about the world, we come to see the implausibility of precisely those metaphysical conceptions that prompted that learning. We come to see that even our loftiest ideas and ideals that point to a realm 'beyond' the world can be explained using only resources we find here, all of those inner drives and needs that our desire for knowledge led us to discover. Rather than challenging the will to truth, Nietzsche takes himself to be displaying the logical outcome of an unrelenting commitment to it. Perspectivism is the heir to metaphysics, the outcome of a loyal adherence to the commitments that underwrite religion and metaphysics themselves. This is why Nietzsche sees the death of God as internally related to Christian morality. Christianity's commitment to truthfulness finally exposes the lie at its very core. What Nietzsche calls the death of God 'is the awe-inspiring *catastrophe* of two thousand years of training in truthfulness that finally forbids itself the *lie involved in belief in God*'[22]. Rather than a futile search for 'absolute truths', Nietzsche thinks that 'what is needed from now on is *historical philosophizing*, and with it the virtue of modesty'[23]. Nietzsche thinks perspectivism displays this kind of modesty.

No longer professing to believe in the Judaeo-Christian God is not the entirety of Nietzsche's concern: 'God is dead; but given the way of men, there may still be caves for thousands of years in which his shadow will be shown. – And we – we still have to vanquish his shadow, too.'[24] The 'shadow' cast by God is long indeed, and it will take considerable effort to ferret out all the ways in which our thinking continues to display God-like tendencies. Nietzsche thinks there are many ways in which our conception of the world shows some allegiance to 'absolutes'. Cause and effect, identity over time, objective moral values: Nietzsche takes up these shadowy remnants at many points in his writings. But there is a further challenge as well. It is not enough to expose the 'human, all too human' origins of lofty metaphysical ideas, nor is it sufficient to debunk metaphysical thinking's pretensions. The grip of such notions is far stronger than a mere critique could loosen (it is something like being shown the props and strings that facilitate a magician's trick; once we return to our seats, we succumb to, and may even be thrilled by, the illusion once again). More than that, merely debunking leaves a void, which offers nothing to take the place of all those views and conceptions so roundly attacked. In keeping with perspectivism, there is no aperspectival point of view, and so one perspective can only be abandoned in order to take up another. 'How foolish it would be to suppose that one only needs to point out this origin and this misty shroud of delusion in order to *destroy* the world that counts for real, so-called "*reality*". We can destroy only as creators.'[25]

▶ Style and self-creation

While Nietzsche's advocacy of perspectivism, as expressing the idea underlying his assertion that God is dead, displays the destructive dimension of existentialism's relation to the history of philosophical and religious thinking, his insistence that 'we can only destroy as creators' points in a more positive, constructive direction. Nietzsche fully recognizes that we are apt to see only destruction on this front, which is why so much of his writing is preoccupied with the threat of what he calls **nihilism**. Nietzsche asks, 'What does nihilism mean? *That the highest values devaluate themselves*. The aim is lacking; "why?" finds no answer.'[26] Nihilism can be understood as an ultimately pathological response to the 'news' of the death of God: insofar as the 'highest values' depended for their currency on a kind of absolute, perspective-free notion of reality and our access to it, the decline of such a notion loosens the grip of any such values. Without anything to take their place, the net effect is a kind of paralysis: there is no reason *why* any one thing is worth doing more than anything else. The question, then, is how we can get beyond this desolate condition.

This is by no means an easy question to answer, but we can make some headway in doing so if we keep in mind two things. First, Nietzsche thinks we need to recognize the way nihilism functions as a kind of transitional stage, where one still takes seriously the need for absolutes. That is, the nihilist is someone who remains convinced that the only thing that *could* give life value and purpose is something that held absolutely; since nothing seems to hold in that way, any sense of value or purpose has been undermined. But this chain of reasoning has not fully absorbed the lesson of Nietzsche's perspectivism, which Nietzsche thinks shows that no values or purposes have ever functioned in that way. And this brings us to the second and more liberating idea: once we recognize that values have always functioned as expressions of our needs and interests, we are now free to re-evaluate things in a way that keeps that fact firmly in view. We no longer need to repress or cover up the real sources of value and purpose, and this, Nietzsche thinks, can get us beyond any nihilistic paralysis to a healthier, more creative way of living.

This kind of transition – from a critical, destructive project to one that is potentially more constructive – is reflected in the structure of Nietzsche's work *The Gay Science*. While the first parts of the book are generally concerned with announcing the 'news' that God is dead and warning of the 'shadow' that news is likely to cast for centuries, the later parts of the book are written in a much more optimistic tone: at aphorism (§) 270 of the book Nietzsche writes: '*What does your conscience say? –* You shall become the person you are.' That Nietzsche depicts this pronouncement as spoken by one's conscience indicates the way it gives voice to a deep truth about oneself to the effect that there is nothing more to who you are beyond whatever it is you become. Whereas Descartes had ushered in the modern era of philosophy with the discovery of a self whose certainty could serve as a basis for all knowledge, Nietzsche, like Kierkegaard before him, encourages a view of the self as an achievement, something we create (and something we may fail to create as well). How are we to understand this idea of self-creation?

There is, to be sure, something inherently paradoxical about the very idea of self-creation: don't I already have to *be* in order for *me* to engage in the activity of creating myself? But if I already have to be, the worry goes, then there is something that I already am, and so the idea of self-creation seems superfluous at best. We might see Nietzsche as attempting to defuse this apparent paradox in a remark that appears shortly after the voice of conscience has spoken. In § 276 of *The Gay Science*, Nietzsche offers as a kind of New Year's resolution an effort 'to learn more and more to see as beautiful what is necessary in things'. There is something deeply puzzling about this appeal to necessity on Nietzsche's part. Haven't I been emphasizing the way his thinking is meant to liberate us from the tyranny of absolutes? How can the notion of self-creation be explained by an appeal to what is necessary? And how does this appeal allay the sense of paradox that besets this whole enterprise?

We might begin to answer these difficult questions by considering what Nietzsche might have in mind as being what is necessary. As we saw with Kierkegaard, if I reflect on my own life, certain things present themselves as having this status: I am a human being, for example, rather than anything else; I have certain physical characteristics, propensities, talents, and abilities. Most of all, I have a past, a life that has been led until now, in which I've done various things and various things have happened to me. That all of this lies in the past means that all of it is something over which I now have no control. Perhaps I could have done something different at the time, avoided a certain **situation** and outcome, but such possibilities are no longer available to me. Such things now carry the force of necessity. The only thing I can do now is take up various attitudes toward the past I have accrued thus far: I can confront my past with an attitude of satisfaction or regret, shame or celebration. And such attitudes are not determined by the flick of a switch: if I find myself feeling ashamed about my past, I cannot just decide to feel differently. But what might alleviate a feeling of shame or regret is carrying on with my life in ways that redeem that shameful or regrettable history. What currently shows up about my past as an occasion for regret can, in light of what I go on to do, come to be viewed as preparatory for something better and more satisfying. I cannot undo the past, but I can change its value and meaning, depending on the broader biography into which those past episodes fit.

The project of self-creation is thus not a matter of fashioning who one is from a completely detached or neutral position. That would indeed be paradoxical, to say the least. Rather, it is a matter of taking stock of who one has become thus far and continuing on in a way that makes, so to speak, a virtue of that necessity. Nietzsche calls this '"giving style" to one's character', which he characterizes in the following terms:

> It is practised by those who survey all the strengths and weaknesses of their nature and then fit them into an artistic plan until every one of them appears as art and reason and even weaknesses delight the eye.[27]

We can see here the way this effort requires an honest assessment of who one already is, and then devising a plan that makes the most of it. Doing so is not easy. Nietzsche continues by noting the 'long practice and daily work' that pulling this off requires, but expending this kind of effort is what is 'needful' in order that 'a human being should attain satisfaction with himself'. To measure the extent to which one has really attained such satisfaction, Nietzsche offers a fantastical test. Coming to understand how this test works will be the final task of this chapter.

▶ Eternal recurrence

Suppose, Nietzsche suggests, you are visited one night – in your 'loneliest loneliness' – by a demon, who informs you that your life will be repeated for all eternity in exactly the same way down to the smallest detail. There will be no variation, no alternative versions. Nietzsche then wonders how you will greet that news: will it fill you with dread and despair or with an overwhelming sense of awe at the demon's powers?

Nietzsche's story about the demon is, after all, just a story. I assume that none of us has ever been visited by such a demon, and there is no reason to believe that anyone ever will. We thus have no reason to believe what Nietzsche reports the demon as saying, that each of our lives will recur in exactly the same way down to the smallest detail for all eternity. How, then, can this notion of **eternal recurrence** serve as 'the greatest weight', as

Nietzsche calls it? What difference can such a parable make if we know that it is only that?

I think Nietzsche hints at the answer to these questions in the final sentences of the section that presents the demon. He writes:

> The question in each and every thing, 'Do you desire this once more and innumerable times more?' would lie upon your actions as the greatest weight. Or how well disposed would you have to become to yourself and to life to crave nothing more fervently than this ultimate confirmation and seal?[28]

Notice that the second question does not presuppose that anyone actually believes the demon's news or has any reason for thinking that what the demon says might be true. Nietzsche instead invokes the idea of longing for the truth of the demon's words. What matters, for Nietzsche, is one's reaction to the idea of eternal recurrence when entertained just as an idea. How would you feel if such a demon visited you? What would your reaction be?

Suppose that the very idea of eternal recurrence fills me with dread. Why might that be? Such a response indicates some form of disappointment with the shape of my life and there is more than one source for it. One source might be *prospective*: in my life, I have been committed to the idea that there was a goal or purpose for my life that would serve to justify it in its entirety. I have made decisions about how to live, about what I ought to do and not do, and so on in light of such a

▲ Nietzsche's summer home in Sils–Maria, Switzerland.

goal. Such a goal would be reached at the end of my life, in the afterlife. By reaching that goal, I would be, in a word, saved. Given such a commitment, the very prospect of eternal recurrence is dreadful to consider, and the dread serves to gauge the strength of that commitment.

So one thing the thought of eternal recurrence measures just by being thought is the extent to which I remain committed to the old scheme of values that Nietzsche thinks are in decline. I still need an absolute to give my life meaning and purpose. If, on the contrary, I find myself longing for the truth of eternal recurrence, that means I recognize and accept that the only thing that gives my life meaning and purpose are the details of that life itself. There is nothing over and above my life that I need or want to redeem it in any way.

I said that there was more than one source of disappointment in the face of the demon's news. The second concerns those details of one's life. This *retrospective* source is the kind of reflective exercise the demon's words prompt: when entertaining the thought of eternal recurrence, I immediately begin to inventory my life as I have led it until now. Are there things I would happily live over again? Are there stretches or episodes that fill me with shame or horror? Which way does the balance tip? We can see in this kind of exercise the way the thought of eternal recurrence functions as a measure of the kind of satisfaction Nietzsche thinks we should strive for. Recall Nietzsche's New Year's resolution wherein he wanted to learn to see what was necessary as beautiful. If one surveys all that one finds both ugly and unchangeable about one's life and the world, learning to do this is far from easy. It is certainly not something one can simply decide to do (consider even a relatively minor moment of shame or embarrassment from your past and try to see it as beautiful). Really coming around to embracing the demon's news as something welcome would entail a dramatic transformation, not only in terms of how one views the past but also in terms of what one goes on to do to redeem the past as it has accumulated until now. The more 'ardently' I long for eternal recurrence, the more satisfied I am with my life as I have led it. And if I find that I cannot long for eternal recurrence, then I've got work to do.

4

Heidegger and the demands of authenticity

And because Dasein is in each case essentially its own possibility, it can, in its very being, 'choose' itself and win itself.

Heidegger, Being and Time

▶ Situating Heidegger

With Martin Heidegger we move into the 20th century and to a figure closer to the epicentre of existentialism as an explicitly conceived and labelled philosophical view. In his public address, published as *Existentialism is a Humanism*, in which Sartre takes ownership of Gabriel Marcel's coinage, Sartre cites Heidegger explicitly as a fellow 'atheistic' existentialist (in contrast to theistically-minded thinkers like Marcel). Despite Sartre's inclusive gesture, we are not quite at the heart of existentialism, and for more than one reason. First, we must bear in mind that Marcel's coinage and Sartre's ownership did not occur until the 1940s, whereas the work Heidegger produced that is most closely associated with existentialism, *Being and Time* and contemporaneous lectures and essays, was written roughly two decades earlier (*Being and Time* was first published in 1927). So Heidegger is still at best an existentialist *avant la lettre*. I say 'at best' because there is some question as to whether Heidegger should be ranked as an existentialist at all. Heidegger was still around when the label began to circulate and he actively resisted its adhering to his thinking, not just his thinking at that time but from the 1920s as well. The kind of 'humanism' that Sartre sees as the core of existentialism is something to which Heidegger claims no allegiance, at least by the late 1940s. Whether Heidegger is reading his own earlier work correctly is another matter and on this question, scholars disagree. I will not consider such disagreements here. Instead, what I will offer here is an existentialist reading of Heidegger, most notably *Being and Time*, without worrying excessively over the precise fidelity of that reading either to Heidegger's original intentions in composing the work or to his work as a whole. Such a reading offers important and illuminating ideas, regardless of whether they are the ones Heidegger wanted to convey.

▶ The question of being

As we have begun to appreciate, an existentialist places a concern with the distinctive character of human existence at the centre of his or her philosophy. Heidegger does so as well, but not without first situating that concern within an even broader one, indeed the broadest possible concern philosophy can have, what Heidegger calls 'the question of being'. For Heidegger, this is *the* question, and not just for him. The dawning of this question in Greek antiquity is what marks the appearance of philosophy in the first place. While the question is in some sense easy to formulate – most simply, 'What is being?' or, more verbosely, 'What is the meaning of being?' – just what the question is asking is far from clear. Heidegger himself acknowledges that the question is a peculiar one that affords little in the way of traction. Part of the problem is that the question has gone dormant for us: we no longer engage with the question sufficiently even to feel perplexed by it. Heidegger sees as one of his principal burdens in *Being and Time* the reawakening of the question of being, so that it grips us in the way he thinks it gripped the ancient Greeks.

▲ Martin Heidegger (1889–1976).

The problem, though, is one of where to begin. How can we begin to grapple with a question that no longer grips us? How can we go about trying to answer it if we are not even sure what it is asking? Before we simply throw our hands up in despair, we may want to stop and think about many of the things we say and do every day. Consider the following contrived but nonetheless plausible things I might hear or say on an ordinary day:

1 Scientists found evidence suggesting that *there is* an asteroid the size of North America orbiting the sun.

2 My son Henry asked me if *there is* a common factor greater than 3 for 153 and 252.

3 I couldn't remember if *there is* a larger C-clamp down in the basement.

4 Margot wondered if *there is* a mouse stealing some of her bunny's food.

Embedded in each of these sentences is a clause that begins with the phrase 'there is' and that phrase in each case is coupled with some kind of entity, broadly speaking. Very roughly, when Heidegger raises the question of being, what he is asking is something along the lines of what 'there is' means in sentences like these. The phrase 'there is' appears to be functioning in the same way in each sentence and so we do not have an obvious or wholesale shift of meaning as we move from sentence to sentence. However, given the array of entities involved in this sampling, we might also wonder whether there is some difference of meaning across them as well. When we say that there is an asteroid and there is a common factor greater than 3 for some pair of numbers, are we making the same *kind* of claim? In some sense we are, in that we are in each case saying that there is something, whether it is an asteroid or a common factor. At the same time, if we start to think about what it comes to for there to *be* an asteroid or for there to *be* a common factor, our sense that we are saying the same kind of thing in each case might falter a bit. Common factors are a markedly different kind of thing from asteroids, and the difference would appear to be a different kind of difference than there is between a pebble and an asteroid. With the latter pair, it makes sense to say that one (the asteroid) is bigger than the other (the pebble), but in what sense is the asteroid bigger than the number 3? There does not appear to be a metric common to both by means of which they might be compared. Asteroids are found in particular regions of space and so their size is a matter of notions like length, width, mass and so on, but none of that pertains to numbers at all: some numbers are larger than others, but that has nothing to do with having a greater length or mass.

The differences among the other examples are more subtle, but still significant. Consider the C-clamp as opposed to the asteroid. Both are spatio-temporal entities and so they can be located and compared fairly straightforwardly, but we should not for that reason assimilate them into one category. The C-clamp is a particular kind of tool that plays a role in the workshop. It was designed and built to serve a purpose (or range of purposes) in building and repairing things. The C-clamp thus has a function and its having one depends upon human activities, upon our using it in various way to do various things. None of that would appear to apply to the asteroid. It has no function and if it plays a role in human activity (as, say, something to be discovered or something to be worried over if it starts to veer close to Earth), that is not a role of our making. We did not design asteroids to play a role in our activities. By contrast, the mouse and the asteroid might pair up rather nicely, as each is a naturally occurring entity (leaving aside the 'designer' mice used in laboratories), but there is a glaring difference as well: the mouse is a living thing, while the asteroid is not.

▶ 'Dasein' and human existence

So once we inquire about that phrase 'there is', we find that there is a great deal in the way of differences and affinities across its uses to sort out. But notice also something else: none of these sentences is especially esoteric or technical and anyone who is more or less fluent in English will be able to produce and consume sentences like these without much difficulty (or for analogues devised in other languages). What this last observation suggests is that perhaps we are not in the dark about the question of being as much as we took ourselves to be. Given this kind of fluency, we all have a certain degree of understanding when it comes to being. Of course, that fluency only goes so far: if pressed to explain just how what it is to be an asteroid differs from what it is to be a common factor, for example, most of us would quickly start to sputter. At the same time, almost all of us readily see the folly of questions such as, 'Is an asteroid bigger or smaller than the number 3?' That we treat such questions as either nonsense or the kind of lame attempts at humour that philosophy professors are wont to make shows that we already have some sense of there being a difference.

For Heidegger, this kind of sensitivity to the categorical affinities and differences with respect to being – a sensitivity displayed in, among other things, the way we produce and understand sentences like the examples above – provides a foothold or point of entry for thinking further about the question of being. Since all of us (and by 'us' I mean all those who possess this kind of sensitivity) have what Heidegger calls an 'understanding of being', then we ourselves provide the point of entry: by developing and making more explicit this largely implicit, non-thematic sensitivity, Heidegger will have thereby gone a long way toward answering the question of being. Notice how quickly we have arrived at the existentialist's trademark concern with the distinctive character of human existence: human existence – what Heidegger refers to by the term **Dasein** and which is generally left untranslated – is distinctive in that it involves an understanding of being. Human beings are beings who are capable, as Heidegger himself shows, of asking and understanding the question of being. But there is a further wrinkle to this: because we are beings who can ask the question of being, we can also question our own being. We are beings whose being 'is an issue' for us. As Heidegger notes emphatically, *'The "essence" of Dasein lies in its existence.'*[29] We confront our own existence as a kind of open question or ongoing concern, and so as something we have to work out or determine in choosing how we live out our lives. At least we *can* choose. Whether we do so in quite the way Heidegger envisions is another matter.

▶ The everyday world and inauthenticity

It will take some stage setting in order to see how we might fail to own up fully to the kind of beings we ourselves are. To begin, consider again the kind of sensitivity to the categorical differences and similarities examined above with respect to being. Although I first laid that out with respect to how we speak and think – with respect to various sentences we might produce and consume – these sensitivities pervade how we act as well. Heidegger remarks very early in *Being and Time* that the 'investigation of Being' he is conducting 'brings to completion ... that understanding of Being which belongs to Dasein and which 'comes alive' in any of its dealings with entities.'[30] (Note that in my own discussions I have not followed the translation cited here in capitalizing 'Being', for two reasons: first, all nouns are capitalized in German, so there is nothing in the original that the translators' choice reflects; second, using 'Being' gives the impression that Heidegger is referring to a special entity, which is something he clearly wants to avoid.)

Heidegger goes on to offer the following succinct example: 'when I open the door, for instance, I use the latch.' It may be difficult to see how reaching out to turn a doorknob could have any philosophical import, but Heidegger thinks there is a lot going on with such everyday 'dealings with entities'. Such dealings manifest the myriad ways in which we understand entities: when I reach out for the doorknob, my understanding of doorknobs 'comes alive'. I show that I know what doorknobs are all about, i.e. that they are *for* grasping and turning *in order to* open a door. I show that I understand how a doorknob is to be used, and so that something counts as using a doorknob correctly (grasping and turning with my hand) rather than incorrectly (such as kicking swiftly with my foot, which might get the door open but would probably break the knob). And understanding all that is part of understanding what a doorknob *is*, namely something for opening, closing and securing doors. Of course, all of this is not something I think much about (except when writing about Heidegger), which indicates that the kind of understanding Heidegger is most interested in is not exactly mental or psychological in the traditional senses of such terms.

We need to be careful here not to think about this kind of understanding that 'comes alive' as parcelled out entity by entity. That is, we should not think that there is some discrete unit of understanding correlated with doorknobs, another with coffee cups, and so on. When we encounter such things in ways that manifest our comprehension of them (making use of them in the appropriate ways), we do so in terms of our grasp of what Heidegger calls a 'totality'. By this, he means that we grasp these entities, both literally and figuratively, in relation to our grasp of other entities to which they are related in various ways, as well as the entire environment in which they have their places. So, for example, when I walk into a classroom to teach my morning class, I may be attending specifically to the lectern as I unpack my notes etc., but in doing so, I am oriented toward the classroom as a whole: the chalkboard, chalk and erasers; the table that holds the lectern; the desks and the students who sit at them, and so on. My use of the lectern is part and parcel of a much more general way of engaging with my surroundings, as well as of understanding myself, namely as a professor going about the business of teaching a course.

Heidegger says that Dasein's way of being is **being-in-the-world**, which means that our most basic forms of understanding, including self-understanding, involve our being caught up in these broad totalities that involve equipment, tasks, projects and roles. We are first and foremost immersed in this world of ongoing activity, and it is in terms of this kind of familiarity with the world that we make sense of everything and anything, at least initially. Notice that Heidegger's insistence on the primacy of being-in-the-world cuts against the grain of the western philosophical tradition, which generally accords to the self or subject a rock-bottom status. Descartes' 'I think, therefore I am' is perhaps the clearest and most famous example of this, and Heidegger devotes considerable effort in *Being and Time* to loosening the grip of Descartes' legacy in philosophy.

I said before that for Heidegger, we are beings who have an understanding of being, and so we are simultaneously beings whose own being is an issue for us. At the same time, that we are beings whose way of being is being-in-the-world means that this fundamental idea is apt to be obscured. Immersed in, and absorbed by, a world of ongoing activity, we are at the same time distracted from the issue of our own lives. Heidegger refers to Dasein in the everyday world as lost or dispersed, scattered about among the various demands that life makes. In a word, Dasein is 'busy' in the way in which we often answer the question of how we're doing with the reply, 'Oh, you know, busy.' Writing in the 1920s, Heidegger is almost presciently attuned to the quickened pace of modern life, whose speed has increased considerably since that time. But we need not construe this way of being lost as a specifically modern phenomenon. Writing in the 19th century, the American writer Henry David Thoreau explains his retreat to Walden Pond as motivated in part by the fear that when he came to die, he would 'discover that [he] had not lived'. Indeed, the contrast between being lost and found pervades the Christian tradition as a whole (just sing a few bars of 'Amazing Grace'), and there is little doubt that Heidegger is drawing extensively from it while trying at the same time to secularize it. Kierkegaard looms large in Heidegger's thinking (recall Kierkgaard's image of the faithless as 'forever running errands in life'), but it should be noted that early in his life, Heidegger was a novitiate in the Jesuit order with the intention of becoming a Catholic priest. Although Heidegger strayed considerably from this initial orientation and affiliation, the structure and significance of religious life continued to occupy him.

▶ Self-discovery and authenticity

The emphasis Heidegger places on the notion of being-in-the-world would appear to leave little room for a positive account of the self or subject. If, as Heidegger insists, our self-understanding and our understanding of the world in which we are immersed are aligned with and determined by one another, then how is that not the end of the matter? *Who* I am would appear to be just this intersection of socially defined roles (professor, husband, father, American etc.), just as who you are is likewise some such intersection. If Heidegger rejects as confused any appeal to an underlying or independent subject, then how can the self be anything more than that socially articulated product? Are we, by Heidegger's account, trapped in the social world in which we find ourselves? That living out our publicly defined lives can have an almost suffocating feel suggests that what is necessary is some kind of radical escape from the 'confines' of our daily existence. Indeed, that suggestion should not be dismissed too lightly. Thoreau felt that escape to be necessary – at least for a period of time – so that he might 'live deliberately'. The painter Paul Gaugin abandoned his family and respectable middle-class life for Tahiti in order to paint, while the writer Samuel Beckett abandoned his native language (English) and wrote his mature and most famous works (such as *Waiting for Godot*) in French. There are no doubt countless less famous instances of such radical turns in a life: consider the near-cliché idea of going out for a packet of cigarettes/a loaf of bread/a carton of milk, and never returning.

That we can feel suffocated by our daily routines – by our own lives – is telling, as it intimates that each of us is indeed something more than an intersection of social roles. Such a feeling, which may take the form of a desire for escape or another form of radical transformation, provides a thread which, if tugged, can lead to the unravelling of the entire socially defined network in which we find ourselves. Heidegger calls this kind of feeling, and the experience to which it gives rise **anxiety**, a kind of crisis that pulls us out of our immersion in everyday life. In anxiety, the everyday world is still there (a bout of anxiety is not a matter of blacking out), but one is no longer engaged by it. Heidegger says that in anxiety 'the totality of involvements ... is, as such, of no consequence'[31]. When I am anxious, my anxiety is not directed toward anything 'out there', nor does whatever there is out there have anything to offer, either to explain or allay my state. This lack of directedness forces a kind of inward turn, not in the sense of introspective soul-searching, but rather a confrontation with the structure and character of one's own existence. Heidegger says: *'That in the face of which one has anxiety is Being-in-the-world as such.'*[32] What I confront in anxiety is precisely the fact of my being the kind of being whose being is an issue, nothing more but also nothing less. I have generally been shying away from much of Heidegger's notoriously novel vocabulary, but here is just a bit of it: in anxiety, I confront my own existence as *thrown possibility*.

My existence is 'thrown' in that I find myself in the midst of a world whose basic contours were not of my choosing and in the midst of an already ongoing life that was not initially – and well beyond that – a matter of choice, but my existence is also 'possibility' in that I experience it as moving forward into an indefinite and still-to-be-determined future. This latter dimension underscores the issue that my ongoing existence consists of for me, but something further lends to this dimension added emphasis and urgency.

That 'something further' is death. We need to be especially careful not to misunderstand what Heidegger means here. He does *not* mean that we become most fully who we are when we are dead, nor that we do so when we try in some way to hasten our own demise along the lines of the motto 'Live fast. Die young. Leave a beautiful corpse.' Furthermore, Heidegger does not think that we should spend our time brooding excessively over our eventually dying, worrying over when and where it might happen, 'how much time we have left' and all of that. None of that is really to the fore. Rather, what is important here is simply what we might call the fact of *finitude*: my life may be indefinitely bounded, but it is inescapably bounded nonetheless. Heidegger says that death is 'ownmost, non-relational, and not to be outstripped', which underscores the idea my death is uniquely mine in that I cannot slough it off onto someone else or in any way overcome or escape it. Other possibilities are relational, by being embedded in broader totalities, and can be outstripped by my forsaking them in favour of others: I used to be a doctor, but then I gave it up; I used to be a golfer, but I lost interest. 'I used to be finite, but ...' does not have any clear sense. At the same time, Heidegger thinks this inescapable fact about us is something that tends to be obscured by everyday life. More than that, it is something that everyday life conspires to obscure. Death in the ordinary sense is an uncomfortable subject, and even when it does come up, it is typically in terms of something that befalls someone else. Others die, but only rarely does this prompt any kind of reflective realization. It is all too easy, Heidegger thinks, to conceive of death either in terms of something that only befalls others or as an indefinitely distant event that is of no concern now. However, finitude is not something lying off in the future, but an ever-present and fundamental feature of one's existence. While we might fantasize that we confront an unlimited array of possibilities, such possibilities are bounded at both ends, so to speak: **thrownness** takes a cut from one side, while death does so from the other.

Overcoming this kind of fantasy is key to Heidegger's conception of **authenticity**. While this is the standard translation of the original *Eigentlichkeit*, the term can be misleading, since being authentic is typically contrasted with being counterfeit (imitation, fake, etc.). However, inauthentic Dasein – our existence as immersed in everydayness – is just as much or genuinely Dasein in that an understanding of being is fully manifest in those ways of engaging with the world. The German, starting with 'Eigen', which means 'own', suggests that authenticity is a matter of self-ownership, i.e. that in becoming authentic I make my own existence most fully that, my own. Acknowledging the thrown, finite character of my existence enables me, Heidegger thinks, to choose among the possibilities arrayed before me. Authenticity is a matter of 'taking over the ground' of my existence not in the sense of controlling it from the bottom up, so to speak, but taking responsibility for its future direction in a way that incorporates and makes sense of what has already been. Heidegger calls this stance or orientation 'anticipatory **resoluteness**'. It is anticipatory in recognizing death as one's 'ownmost possibility', and resolute in choosing on the basis of that possibility, rather than fleeing back into the dispersed, distracted bustle of everyday life.

Escaping can thus go in a number of directions: our everyday existence, to which we may feel confined, is at the same time something *to* which we escape to avoid the painful truth about ourselves as thrown finite beings. If I keep my head down and keep myself busy, I can avoid facing up to the issue of my own life. While anxiety does involve a kind of wrenching free from everyday life, it need not involve a literal departure of the kind involved in various forms of self-imposed exile. To be authentic in Heidegger's sense, I need not exchange my current world – my current culture – for another. Simply exchanging one for another could just as easily allow for immersion and distraction all over again. Instead, authenticity is a matter of how I relate myself to my world, the one in which I find myself or the one I find myself seeking out instead. What is crucial here is my indeed making it *my* world, in that I take ownership of my way of moving ahead in it. For some, doing this may require the kind of wholesale change that we see in the lives of Thoreau, Gaugin and Beckett, but one can be authentic – fully own up to who one is and how one is – without leaving home.

5

Sartre and self-responsibility

We are left alone and without excuse.

Sartre, Existentialism is a Humanism

▶ Back to where it would begin

Nearly a hundred years after the death of Søren Kierkegaard, we arrive at the official beginning of existentialism. As I have noted already, existentialism is a peculiarly structured movement or tradition in philosophy, since it encompasses numerous thinkers only retroactively and, in many cases, posthumously. Now, with Jean-Paul Sartre, we can speak of an existentialist without qualification or caveat, as he himself used that label for himself and his philosophy, albeit reluctantly at first. By the time Sartre adopted the label, he was already a well-established figure in French intellectual circles, having written several works of philosophy, including the elegantly slender *The Transcendence of the Ego* and the imposingly hefty *Being and Nothingness*, as well as novels, plays and short stories. We will consider some of this work in the discussion to follow, but we will begin with the work that serves to found existentialism.

▶ Deciphering a slogan

Delivered shortly after the end of the Second World War, Sartre's public address, later published as *Existentialism is a Humanism*, can be considered the coming-out party for the view, replete with banner-ready slogans and a spirited defence against various adversaries. Let us begin with the primary slogan Sartre offers, which may be taken as definitive of existentialism in general: 'Existence precedes essence'. As slogans go, it is not especially catchy, couched as it is in philosophically loaded vocabulary (compare Nietzsche's inflammatory 'God is dead'). Rather than raising our fists in raucous approval, we are far more likely to react to Sartre's slogan by scratching our heads and asking what it means.

It might be best to start with the last word – essence – and work our way back. The term 'essence' has a very long history in philosophy and we cannot hope here to follow its many twists and turns through the ages. But we can get a rough idea of what the term connotes: when we speak of something's essence, we are referring to what something is. While essence concerns what something is, existence pertains to something's actuality, *that* it is rather than *what* it is. The two notions are traditionally taken to be separable: I can specify and ponder an essence while bracketing the question of whether that kind of thing really exists or has 'instances'. For example, I can ask and answer the question, 'What is a unicorn?' while leaving open whether there are any such creatures, or even denying that there are. A substantive answer to the question, 'What is a unicorn?' allows, and leaves open, the question, 'Are there unicorns?'

We are now left to interrogate this middle term. To get a feel for what 'precedes' means here, it will be helpful to think of Sartre's slogan by way of contrast. Sartre's slogan is a reversal of the standard or traditional view of the relation between existence and essence. I noted above that essence and existence have typically been

▲ Jean-Paul Sartre (1905–80).

understood as separable and in a way that gives pride of place to essence. In that way, essence is prior to, takes precedence over, existence. We can begin to see how much is packed into the notion of precedence if we consider Sartre's own example of something for which essence clearly precedes existence: the paper knife or letter opener. The choice is perhaps a bit dated, as more and more of our 'mail' arrives electronically, but the particular example is not especially important: any human tool would serve to illustrate Sartre's point. I should also warn that any example along these lines incurs the same liabilities as well, which we will consider in due course.

The paper knife, like most other tools, is an item that someone, or some group of people, deliberately made. The paper knife is something that someone had in mind and created according to a specific plan and for a particular purpose (or range of purposes). We can think of that plan and attendant purposes as the paper knife's essence, since they specify very clearly *what* it is. That the essence of the paper knife is bound up with the plan and purposes gives us one very clear sense of its precedence over existence: the plan comes before the existence of any given paper knife in time. Temporal or chronological precedence is only one way in which the essence of the paper knife has priority over the existence of any particular paper knife. Suppose I pick up one such paper knife and ask *why* there is such a thing. I am not here just asking why there is a paper knife in this place (on the kitchen counter rather than the table, say) but why there is such a thing at all. My why-question is asking something like how there came to be this paper knife and any other. Although there might be a lengthy story to tell about the origins of this paper knife, including all the details of its manufacture, it is clear that the plan for it – the paper knife's design – will figure prominently in that story. There is this paper knife, and all others of its kind, because someone designed and built it. So precedence in this case means *explanatory* precedence: we explain the existence of the paper knife in part by invoking its essence.

There is at least one more sense of precedence to ferret out. Consider the following: having received a letter I wish to read, I reach for the paper knife. Rather than cleanly slicing open the envelope, the paper knife leaves a jagged, shredded opening. In this case, the paper knife's performance leaves me feeling irritated. If we consider the source of my irritation, we can say it stems in part from my having an expectation regarding the performance of the paper knife. Moreover, that expectation is legitimate, since I was putting the paper knife to its intended use. (Compare my taking the paper knife out to prune my azaleas; I certainly would not be entitled to complain of its shortcomings on that front.) There is something the paper knife is supposed to do – slice open envelopes and the like – and that gives me or anyone else a basis for evaluating any particular paper knife. What the paper knife is supposed to do is the thing that its essence specifies, and so we can say that the essence takes *evaluative* precedence over any particular paper knife.

Now that we have a clearly delineated case of essence preceding existence, we can consider just what Sartre is claiming by reversing the standard formula. Sartre motivates the claim via an appeal to atheism: when it comes to human existence, there is no being that plays a role analogous to that of the designer in the case of the paper knife. Since there is no designer or creator to have conceived of human existence beforehand, there is no prior essence that takes any kind of precedence (temporal, explanatory, evaluative) over human existence. As Sartre puts it, 'if God does not exist, there is at least one being in whom existence precedes essence'[33]. If we stop for a moment and ponder what Sartre says here, at least two worries come to the fore: first, we might note that Sartre has offered us a pretty big 'if'. To be confident that existence really precedes essence for human beings, don't we need to know or have shown that God really does not exist? Otherwise, we are just left with this conditional statement and perhaps some people who believe that God does not exist and so believe that existence precedes essence. Second, what are we to make of Sartre's 'at least'? I noted before that Sartre's choice of examples of where essence precedes existence has shortcomings and now we might begin to see how that is so. If Sartre's claim hinges on an appeal to atheism, then it will be hard to see how the notion of existence preceding essence designates something distinctive or special about *human* existence. For any naturally occurring thing – for anything not deliberately manufactured by human beings – there will be no creator (or Creator) to have conceived of it beforehand and so no prior essence. Sartre's slogan will then apply as much to oak trees and snow leopards, squirrels and starfish as it does to human existence. And that seems like an unwanted conclusion. (Just why it is unwanted will become clear when we see what other ideas are bound up with the idea of existence preceding essence.)

I think there is a way of addressing this second worry that will serve to take care of the first as well. When Sartre first offers the slogan we have been considering, he also offers a second one. What existentialists have in common, Sartre claims, is the 'belief that existence precedes essence; or, if you prefer, that subjectivity must be our point of departure'[34]. A connection between these two formulations is hardly obvious, but it is important to see how for Sartre they are bound up with one another. Indeed, the second formulation serves to ground the first. In *Being and Nothingness*, Sartre argues at length that our existence has a special structure – the structures of what Sartre calls the **for-itself** – because we are conscious (and self-conscious) beings. That is, we are beings for whom existence precedes essence *because* we are beings who are aware of, or confront, our own existence as something ongoing and in need of determination. The very idea of **consciousness** involves the notion of what Sartre calls **nihilation**. There are many aspects to this notion, but roughly the idea is that as conscious, self-aware beings, we are continually in the process of nihilating our own existence: we are aware of ourselves as no longer what we were and not yet what we will be. (Any entity existing through time has a 'no longer' and a 'not yet', of course, but those are not available to the entity unless that entity is self-aware in the way we are.) For Sartre, the phenomenon of nihilation – including self-nihilation – implies the falsity of determinism when it comes to human existence. (Sartre on occasion declares determinism to be 'unthinkable' or 'impossible' when applied to our ongoing conscious lives.) Hence, there can be no prior essence that in any way determines in advance the shape of human existence.

Notice that we have now addressed the two worries raised above. First, Sartre's claim that existence precedes essence does not depend on the truth of atheism. This is perhaps why, after emphasizing his atheist credentials throughout the address, Sartre says at the very end that 'existentialism is not so much an atheism in the sense that it would exhaust itself attempting to demonstrate the non-existence of God; rather, it affirms that even if God were to exist, it would make no difference'[35]. That latter affirmation would be extremely puzzling – if not incoherent – if the defining claim of existentialism *required* the truth of what the atheist espouses. Second, we can see that even if we do affirm Sartre's atheism, the notion of existence preceding essence does not generalize wildly. The claim pertains only to beings whose existence includes the structures of subjectivity we find in the case of human beings. Sartre's 'at least' leaves open that there may be other such beings besides us – there may be beings in galaxies far away who enjoy the same kind of self-awareness as we do – but that too is not something Sartre exhausts himself trying to establish or refute.

So to say that in the case of human existence 'existence precedes essence' means that there is no answer to the question of what or who we are in advance of how we actually go about our existence. Each of us is the 'ensemble' of our choices, actions and situations, and since this ensemble is continually developing as we continue to live, there is no complete description of it until those lives have finished. Ironically, there is no complete 'me' until I am no longer. Contrary to the standard view, there is no hope of separating essence and existence, as there is no essence to ponder prior to, or apart from, how any of us actually goes about his or her life. But there is more to Sartre's claims than just these senses of incompleteness and inseparability. The history of the paper knife is also unfinished until it is destroyed, but with the paper knife there is a kind of norm or standard that governs that history. Again, there is something the paper knife is supposed to do. To deny a prior essence in the case of human existence is to deny that there is any such 'supposed to' that is binding on us as human beings. According to Sartre, 'we have neither behind us, nor before us, in the luminous realm of values, any means of justification or excuse. We are left alone and without excuse'.[36] Let us see what else is involved in this solitude.

▶ Freedom, anguish and responsibility

That Sartre connects the notions of existence preceding essence and subjectivity to a rejection of determinism indicates the intimate connection between these notions and that of **freedom**. Sartre maintains that we are 'condemned to be free'. Whether we look back to medieval conceptions of human freedom as testimony to God's benevolence or consider more contemporary appeals to the importance of independence and autonomy, Sartre's coupling of freedom and condemnation is surely jarring. For Sartre, human freedom is not all sweetness and light. That 'we are left alone and without excuse' indicates the darker dimensions of human freedom.

We are condemned to be free because our freedom is grounded in a kind of 'un-freedom': being free beings is not something any of us freely chose to be. We simply find ourselves to be beings who have to choose for ourselves, but this is not something we got to choose in the first place. We never had the opportunity to choose to be a kind of thing that lacked this sort of freedom, such as a snow leopard or an oak tree.

It is difficult to overestimate the extent of our responsibility. Condemned to be free, each of us 'carries the weight of the whole world' on his or her shoulders. The responsibility of the for-itself is 'overwhelming', as it is only through the for-itself that 'it happens that there is a world'.[37] Sartre goes so far as to say that in life 'there are no *accidents*'.[38] Even in the extreme case of the outbreak of war, my responsibility is indelible: 'If I am mobilized in a war, this war is *my* war; it is in my image and I deserve it.' Sartre explains these harsh pronouncements by noting that 'I could always get out of it by suicide or by desertion.'[39] If I do not get out of it, then I have thereby chosen it. In light of Sartre's gloss on responsibility as an awareness of being the incontestable author of something, it is hard to see how I am responsible for the war just by being mobilized. I may be complicit in the ongoing waging of the war, but surely it would go on with or without me. Moreover, Sartre's appeal to desertion and suicide do not really suffice to account for my responsibility, since those choices are made in the face of an already unfolding war: I choose to desert because war has broken out; I choose to take my life to avoid going to war. While I may be able to choose how I respond to those conditions – and so what significance those conditions have for me – my choosing does not extend to the entirety of those conditions themselves. Sartre perhaps goes too far with this example, but I think the main point here is that there is no principled way of drawing a clear limit to my responsibility. Attempting to do so is apt to look evasive, a way of finding excuses for acting in ways that are in fact optional for me.

Responsibility does not just run deep for Sartre, but wide as well: 'And when we say that man is responsible for himself, we do not mean that he is responsible only for his own individuality, but that he is responsible for all men.'[40] The extension of responsibility to 'all men' is no doubt puzzling. How can what I choose to do or be have a bearing on or make a difference to someone on the other side of the world? And likewise, how can I be held responsible for choices made by that faraway someone? While there may be cases where particular choices have an impact or consequences far removed from their occurrence – choices made in the context of a global economy might be cited here – these cases involve very complicated connections and dependencies that are unlikely to be present across the board. Sartre himself writes of a kind of 'direct responsibility toward the other men who will be directly affected by' a decision, as in the case of a commanding office issuing an order to his troops, but that kind of 'direct' connection usually dissipates with time and distance[41]. Thus it is hard to see how my choosing as such generalizes in such a way that 'in choosing myself, I choose man'[42]. A more modest but nonetheless significant way of understanding Sartre here might be discerned in his remark that 'our actions ... create an image of man as we think he ought to be'[43]. In choosing and acting as we do, each of us is at the same time an example that others might emulate. Even if we do not demand that others choose and act as we do, we are at least acting in ways that others may follow. I may try to evade this kind of exemplarity by seeing my choices as only involving me and even as choices I expressly don't want others to make. Sartre himself offers a version of Kant's famous example of lying: in choosing to lie to get something I want or need, I rely on others by and large not lying. If lying were to become too widespread, the efficacy of lying would break down. So, in effect, in choosing to lie, I am implicitly demanding that others do not do so. This kind of evasion is thus a way of denying the freedom of others: if I treat my choices as exceptional, I am thereby trying to restrict others in their choices and actions. Ultimately, these kinds of restrictions have a way of rebounding, as my freedom turns out to be reciprocally bound to the freedom of others: 'I cannot set my own freedom as a goal without also setting the freedom of others as a goal.'[44]

We are condemned to be free insofar as we are burdened with this tremendous sense of responsibility. We experience this burden as what Sartre calls **anguish**. Recall Heidegger's appeal to the fundamental role of anxiety as revealing Dasein's 'that it is and has to be'. Although not equivalent, we can see a kinship between Heidegger's notion and Sartre's. We feel anguish in that we confront our own existence as something to be worked out or determined and where we ourselves are the ones who have to determine it. Being 'left alone, without excuses' is not exactly a pleasant feeling. Anguish attends this absence of determination and in more than one way. First, recall Sartre's rejection of determinism. In the standard opposition between freedom of the will and determinism, champions of freedom of the will conceive of it as a special kind of power, the agent's power to choose free from any prior determination. Sartre's conception of freedom shares some of this original idea, as his conception of responsibility bears out. In *Being and Nothingness*, he includes in his notion of responsibility the 'ordinary sense' of an awareness of being the 'incontestable author' of an event. At the same time, the experience of this lack of determination is fraught with anguish since the effectiveness of this 'power' requires continual renewal. That is, the absence of determination extends to my own prior decisions and resolutions. Recall Sartre's conception of subjectivity as involving a kind of continual 'nihilation' of oneself: my past shows up to me as a 'no longer', while my future shows up as a 'not yet'. While yesterday I may have resolved to act or refrain from acting in some way today, I now apprehend that resolution as a kind of inert object with no special ability to make me do something at the present time. Sartre gives the example of a gambler who had sworn off gambling once and for all, only to be drawn once again to the gaming tables. 'What the gambler apprehends at this instant ... is the permanent rupture in determinism; it is nothing which separates him from himself.'[45] The 'rupture' the gambler apprehends accounts for his anguish in the face of further opportunities to gamble: he experiences his prior resolve fading into the past as he reaches for a stack of chips.

▶ Bad faith

The continual nihilation of oneself accounts for a further and pervasive sense of anguish. Unlike what Sartre calls the **in-itself** – things which just are what they are – beings whose existence involves the structures of the for-itself lack this kind of stable identity over time. As a being whose existence precedes my essence I can never just *be* something. Human existence has a kind of paradoxical structure: a human being is what it is not and is not what it is. We are an unstable combination of what Sartre calls **facticity**, which corresponds to our having-been, and **transcendence**, our future-directed surpassing of what we were. As we live out our lives, we are continually surpassing – nihilating – who we have been, but each of us is surpassing a specific having-been, a particular life-history, bodily make-up, and so forth. That this combination tends toward instability accounts for the anguished character of human existence, as well as various 'patterns' of human activity that seek to cover over this kind of anguish. Sartre calls these patterns **bad faith**.

As with anguish, Sartre's notion of bad faith bears traces of Heidegger's notion of inauthenticity. However, bad faith more closely follows Kierkegaard's earlier notion of despair. Recall that Kierkegaard characterizes despair as an 'imbalance' between the two 'factors' involved in selfhood. Sartre's notions of facticity and transcendence are two such factors or dimensions, whose 'coordination', to use Sartre's term, is hardly automatic. There is something despairing about the characters in Sartre's richly drawn examples of bad faith in *Being and Nothingness*: in each case, the person exemplifying bad faith cannot bring him- or herself to acknowledge fully some vital aspect of the situation and his or her own role in it. Such a failure of acknowledgment constitutes a kind of evasion: 'The goal of bad faith ... is to put oneself out of reach; it is an escape.'[46] The young woman who lets her hand lie inert in the grasp of her young suitor, neither withdrawing it nor reciprocating his gesture, hides herself from the erotically charged situation in which she herself is complicit. The man who refuses to draw out the (painfully obvious) implications of his repeated liaisons with other men is thereby trying to escape from his own past actions and choices. He capitalizes on the contrast between the in-itself and the for-itself. Since he cannot *be* a homosexual in the way that a table *is* a table, he tells himself and others that he cannot really be a homosexual at all. (Like the paper knife, Sartre's example of the agonized homosexual is also becoming dated as the stigma associated with same-sex relations continues to diminish.) The man in effect uses his undeniable transcendence as a way to try to efface or disown his facticity altogether, and that is bad faith.

Sartre's most famous example of bad faith is the café waiter. Observing his overly precise, overly attentive manner, Sartre concludes that he is playing at being a waiter. The waiter treats being a waiter as a role to perform – a kind of shtick – and is in a very real way absent from the performance. It can be unsettling to talk to someone caught up in such a role, as one keeps waiting to discern the person behind the performance. Without such discernment, there is little that is conversational in such verbal exchanges; instead, there is a script, a set of lines, that the character utters, and one can in turn begin to feel like a character as well, with one's own scripted set of lines. (Here we can get a glimpse at the way one's freedom is not a purely individual affair.) In this way, we can see the waiter as putting himself 'out of reach'. You do not talk to 'him', only to 'the waiter'. This may suggest a sense of power on the waiter's part, but we must also note that he is the one who has been reduced to a kind of rigid performance and this marks his acquiescence to a kind of societal demand or pressure. He plays the part that has been meted out to him and in a way that lives up to the expectations of his customers and those for whom he works.

▶ 'Hell is other people'

Bad faith can be understood as a kind of imbalance, a 'tipping of the scales' overly toward either facticity or transcendence. I am in bad faith when my existence approximates that of a thing – of the in-itself – but I am also in bad faith when I act as though I were beyond my past and my situation entirely. But there is another kind of balancing act in play when it comes to bad faith.

Sartre introduces the example of the waiter – the second of his three examples in the bad faith chapter of *Being and Nothingness* – by introducing two further aspects or dimensions of human existence whose interplay can be fraught with difficulty. These two dimensions are what Sartre calls *being-for-itself* and *being-for-others*. (Although the example of the waiter makes this interplay vivid, I do not think we should understand it to have been absent in the earlier example of the young woman and her suitor, as there is clearly a tension between how the young woman sees herself in the situation and how she is seen by the suitor.) I should emphasize here that Sartre disallows any kind of first-person authority in this interplay, such that my self-understanding automatically trumps the way others understand me. He notes the 'equal dignity of being, possessed by my being-for-others and by my being-for-myself'[47]. Both are equally mine, as being-for-others involves how I experience myself as presented to and for others. This equality, Sartre further notes, 'permits a perpetually disintegrating synthesis and a perpetual game of escape from the for-itself to the for-others and from the for-others to the for-itself'[48]. Notice again Sartre's appeal to 'escape', as something made possible by this 'perpetually disintegrating synthesis'. How I am for others and how I am for myself are both aspects of my existence whose alignment is continually in danger of coming apart. I may escape from myself, so as to be how others perceive me to be – I become the overbearing waiter, the class clown, the helpless victim, the shameless flirt – but I can also resist or recoil from these ways of being understood, and so retreat into myself once more.

This kind of push and pull between being-for-self and being-for-others is rooted in Sartre's understanding of the foundations for all interpersonal relations: what he calls simply 'the look'. In *Being and Nothingness*, Sartre describes the way the very presence of another person serves to alter fundamentally my experience of a setting or situation. Prior to noting that presence, my environment is just that – mine – and so is arrayed before me and organized entirely in terms of my perspective. The presence of the other introduces a new perspective, lines of sight that trace back to him or her rather than to me. The environment now becomes a scene or a spectacle for him/her, and the way it is available for him/her is unavailable to me: the other has 'stolen the world from me'[49]. The world is still there, but fundamentally changed: 'Everything is in place; everything still exists for me; but everything is traversed by an invisible flight and fixed in the direction of a new object.'[50] My setting – as no longer just *my* setting – is thus charged with a new meaning or significance when my solitary enjoyment of it is disrupted and there is something immediately threatening inherent in that new significance.

This sense of threat – what starts out as the threat of losing my world – intensifies dramatically when the line of sight emanating from the other encompasses me. It is bad enough when the other sees things from a different perspective; it is far worse when I experience myself as being seen by the other. In being seen – in being subjected to 'the look' – I become self-conscious in an entirely different way. In my solitude, I had been taking in my surroundings, absorbed in my own thoughts and occupied with my own activities and plans. When seen, that absorption is interrupted, as I now become aware of how what I am doing looks to someone else. I might begin to worry that what I am doing looks stupid or silly or embarrassing (perhaps I was singing as I walked or happily playing with a yo-yo and now I feel stupid for doing so). I may try to 'act cool' or pretend to be indifferent; I have to decide whether to be friendly, offer a greeting or engage in conversation. What had been just my own activity now has a performative and objective dimension. Indeed, I become the object of another's gaze; I am experiencing myself *as* an object *for* another. For Sartre, the look serves to objectify me: when I experience myself being seen, my existence takes on a kind of solidity it had been lacking. My awareness of my body and my activity undergoes a fundamental shift. At the same time, anything the other can do to me is something I can do to him or her. I may experience myself as being seen by the other, but the other in turn may experience him- or herself as being seen by me. I can thus break the hold of the other's look by subjecting him/her to the look instead. I walk toward the other person whose presence had disrupted my solitude: he/she looks at me intently and I falter, averting my gaze down and away from him/her. When that happens, I am dominated, an object for the other. Now suppose it goes the other way: I look intently and he/she looks away. In that case, I have asserted, indeed reclaimed, a kind of mastery over the situation: he/she is *my* object in *my* situation. The look initiates a kind of struggle between self and other involving the continual assertion and loss of power of one over the other. Sartre's conception of interpersonal relations is fundamentally agonistic. (It is telling that there is in *Being and Nothingness* a lengthy discussion of sadism, but nothing on friendship.) Given his account of the look in *Being and Nothingness*, it is unsurprising that the most memorable line in his play *No Exit* is 'hell is other people'. The play vividly dramatizes the perpetual see-sawing in interpersonal relations between dominating and being dominated. Trapped for eternity in one small room without even the relief of sleep (and, tellingly, without any mirrors in which to see themselves), the three characters have no need of any further agent or instrument of torture.

The 'equal dignity' of being-for-self and being-for-others implies both our need for and resistance to others. (Recall Oscar Wilde's quip that the only thing worse than being talked about is not being talked about.) Since existence precedes essence, I am nothing more than the 'ensemble' of my choices, actions and projects, but the status of that ensemble is determined in part by its reception by others. I am not just what I want to be or what I take myself to be, since what I am is beholden to how I am perceived by others. This is why Sartre says that 'the man who becomes aware of himself directly in the *cogito* also perceives all others, and he does so as the condition of his own existence'[51]. Despite the agonistic character of much of Sartre's account, we can nonetheless discern a more positive dimension. The push and pull of the look, wherein I feel subjected to you but may subject you in turn, might be overcome through a more reciprocal form of recognition. I affirm your status as a free being, which allows you to affirm mine, and vice versa. Indeed, each of us needs the other's affirmation in order to experience ourselves fully as free beings: when 'I have acknowledged that existence precedes essence, and that man is a free being who, under any circumstance, can only ever will his freedom, I have at the same time acknowledged that I must will the freedom of others'[52]. Hell may be other people, but they are an indispensible part of our salvation as well.

Sartre and self-responsibility

6

Camus and the absurd hero

Thus I draw from the absurd three consequences, which are my revolt, my freedom, and my passion.

Camus, 'The Myth of Sisyphus'

▶ Odd man out?

We have seen throughout our discussion that, apart from Sartre, identifying a thinker as an existentialist can be a delicate matter. The retroactive application of the label accounts for some of the difficulty, but Heidegger provided us with an example of active resistance. In the case of the Algerian-born French writer Albert Camus, we again have reason to qualify considerably his affiliation with existentialism. Camus was a near-contemporary of Sartre, emerging as a literary figure in the early 1940s with the publication of the novel *The Stranger* and the philosophical essay 'The Myth of Sisyphus'. Sartre wrote a lengthy commentary on *The Stranger* that appeared in early 1943. Although Sartre is clearly impressed with the novel and devotes considerable effort to illuminating the complexity beneath the sometimes disarmingly simple prose, he also questions Camus's philosophical credentials. Remarking on 'The Myth of Sisyphus', Sartre notes that 'Camus seems to pride himself on quoting Jaspers, Heidegger and Kierkegaard, whom he seems not to have always truly understood.'[53] Sartre and Camus became personally acquainted around that time and moved in the same circles for several years. However, when Camus's later book *The Rebel* received an unfavourable review in Sartre's journal, *Les Temps Modernes*, in the early 1950s, a very public and very acrimonious falling-out ensued.

Although their close association prior to their feud has had a tendency to identify the two thinkers in the popular imagination as fellow existentialists, we should still be wary of such an identification. For one, Camus himself in 'The Myth of Sisyphus' juxtaposes unfavourably what he calls 'the existential attitude' with his own response to the realization that life is absurd. At the same time, Camus's characterization of this attitude is highly selective (he mentions only Kierkegaard, Jaspers and the Russian thinker Leo Chestov) and at times rather obscure (don't forget Sartre's condescension). Nonetheless, the very attempt at a contrast indicates that Camus wishes to view existentialism from a perhaps nearby but still outside perspective. Correlatively, Simone de Beauvoir, in a 1945 essay, 'Existentialism and Popular Wisdom', defends existentialism against the charge of pessimism in part by citing the prevalence in 'popular wisdom' of degraded views of the human condition, remarking at one point: 'Men didn't wait for the "Mythe de Sisyphe" to think that life was, as Shakespeare said, "a tale told by an idiot"; in other words an absurd adventure.'[54] It seems clear that de Beauvoir here lumps Camus in with the kind of commonplace views with which existentialism proper is to be contrasted.

These considerations suggest that we would go wrong were we to assimilate overly Camus's ideas to those we have encountered in previous chapters. At the same time, I am not persuaded that Camus should be excluded entirely from a discussion of existentialism, especially at an introductory level. For one thing, Camus has been identified with existentialism for decades. While this does not *ipso facto* make him an existentialist, some explanation is required of why this popular identification is nonetheless problematic; providing such

▲ Albert Camus (1913–60).

an explanation in turn requires some detailed attention to his views. Moreover, even if not a bona fide variety of existentialism, Camus's views are close enough to existentialism to warrant attention as, variously, a challenge or a cautionary tale. What I mean here is that Camus and the more canonical existentialist thinkers share a great deal in the way of presuppositions, especially when it comes to being suspicious of more traditional conceptions of meaning and value: God is dead as much for Camus as for Nietzsche and Sartre.

For Camus the only legitimate response to this 'event' is striving to be an *absurd hero*; anything more smacks of nostalgia or what he calls 'philosophical suicide'. If canonical existentialism does indeed have something more to offer, the challenge Camus raises is one of demanding to know just how it is entitled to do so.

▶ Absurdity

Camus's 'The Myth of Sisyphus' begins with what he considers to be the 'one truly serious philosophical problem, and that is suicide'[55]. The principal task of philosophy is to judge 'whether life is or is not worth living'[56]. Camus refers to everything else philosophy might be thought to deal with as mere 'games'[57]. We can see Camus as approaching the problem of suicide by wrestling with the following conditional statement:

If life has no meaning, then life is not worth living.

Or, in other words:

If life has no meaning, then suicide is legitimate.

There is something intuitively plausible about these conditionals, as we tend to see the worth of one's life as bound up with its meaning. If we really were to find our lives to be meaningless, then it would seem to follow that those lives are not worth living, that we would be better off calling it quits, packing it in, departing the scene as quickly as possible. One of Camus's principal aims in 'The Myth of Sisyphus' is to sever the connection between the two parts of the conditional statement.

Camus wants to affirm that life indeed has no meaning, but argue that life is nonetheless worth living (even, as we shall see, more so). Put a bit more cautiously, what Camus argues is that even if one has reached the conclusion – has convinced oneself, as I think he has – that life has no meaning, it does not follow that life is not worth living; suicide is thus not a legitimate response to life's lack of meaning.

The idea that life has meaning is to be contrasted with the idea that life is absurd. Although Camus gives a kind of formal definition of **absurdity** in the essay, he treats the notion as a kind of umbrella concept covering such notions as pointlessness, inexplicability, irrationality and being without justification. Indeed, he begins by enumerating various feelings or intimations of absurdity before stepping back to treat the notion proper. Such feelings lay 'the foundations' and 'that is all'[58]. The kind of feelings Camus has in mind all arise from the disruption of a previously enjoyed complacency. As he puts it, 'the stage sets collapse'[59] and that can prompt a 'definitive awakening'[60]. Recall our discussion of Heidegger: in going about our lives, we are absorbed by and dispersed among our various routines and the demands they make up on us. My alarm goes off, I get up, go to the bathroom, wake the kids, make breakfast, get the kids on the bus, get ready for work, teach my classes, and so on. Each day comes to an end with my getting ready for bed and going to sleep, only to have my alarm go off again the next morning so that I can start all over again. Most of the time, I am carried along by the demands this routine imposes. But as we saw with Heidegger's notion of anxiety – to which Camus refers here – the spell cast by this routine can be broken. For no apparent reason whatsoever, I may on some particular day, on some particular occasion, suddenly experience a kind of wake-up call where I ask myself, 'What is all this about?'

There are other ways in which the 'stage set' might collapse, according to Camus, where my daily routines are not the primary focus. Feelings of the absurd can be aroused by encounters with the natural world as well. Consider the changing seasons. There can be something charming, even beautiful, about winter. The winter landscape is often perceived as an almost magical transformation that we characterize in ways that emphasize the delight we take in how it appears. But such appearances quickly fade if I am stranded in the snow. On such occasions, the whole notion of a winter wonderland feels like a facade, almost a kind of joke. On such occasions, 'the primitive hostility of the world rises up to face us across millennia'[61]. But even these appearances are facades in their own way too. Hostility suggests a kind of agency on the world's part, but this is wrong. The ice, snow and cold do not have any kind of plan or purpose with respect to me. We can on such occasions be struck by the 'denseness and strangeness of the world'[62], by the thought that we are forced to live out our lives – or lose them – amidst a natural world that has nothing to do with us at all. When we are so struck, feelings of absurdity are thereby aroused.

Skidding cars, falling trees, and torrential rains are not the only kinds of things that can reveal a kind of strangeness and density beneath what had been familiar facades. 'Men, too, secrete the inhuman.'[63] Camus gives a now dated example of watching a man carry on a conversation behind the glass of a telephone booth. With his voice muted, 'you see his incomprehensible dumb show: you wonder why he is alive.'[64] In a detached frame of mind, all kinds of activities that we normally find natural and familiar can take on a more alien appearance. If I step back and just watch someone eating, the whole affair can begin to look bizarre. The chewing and chomping, the mixing of food and saliva, swallowing and digesting, only to be excreted as waste: what is the point of such a repulsive exercise? (Sex fares no better when subjected to such detached scrutiny.) Indeed, pretty much anything can begin to look strange viewed with a kind of squint – choosing shoes, painting one's nails, getting a haircut, shopping for deodorant and toothpaste, doing the dishes. All the things that usually strike us as matter of course – indeed, they hardly strike us in any way at all – can suddenly seem like the oddest things in the world. They can, in other words, begin to seem absurd.

In enumerating the intimations of absurdity, Camus saves what he takes to be the best for last: 'I come at last to death and the attitude we have toward it.'[65] What is striking here is primarily the *absence* of an attitude: 'Yet one will never be sufficiently surprised that everyone lives as if no one "knew."'[66] Again, Heidegger is lurking in the background here insofar as he thinks that everydayness involves a kind of cover-up of Dasein's finitude or mortality. The problem here, according to Camus, is the way any attempt to acquire knowledge is inevitably thwarted. There is 'no experience of death'[67] in any proper sense. One may perhaps be awake as one's life gives out, but then that is it: whatever was experienced in those last moments were still moments prior to death, but there is no experience of death itself, since one's life and experience have thereby ceased. If there is some kind of life after our earthly demise, replete with a whole new set of experiences, that does not do any of us still living any good: none of us can lay claim to such experiences and there has been thus far no credible means of communication from any such 'beyond'. To confront death is to confront merely a darkness or a blank, but even these terms are going too far: darkness and blankness are still a kind of experience, where one sees nothing but darkness or blankness. That all of our lives inevitably culminate in such a cannot-be-experienced end of experience casts a kind of absurd pall over our lives as a whole.

Camus insists that these feelings or intimations of absurdity are not themselves the notion of the absurd. Again, they only 'lay the foundations'. Generally speaking, the absurd always involves the clash – even the contradiction – between two elements. No one thing can in and of itself be absurd. A dead chicken is not by itself absurd, nor is a knight in shining armour, but a knight hitting someone with a dead chicken is absurd. This example, taken from *Monty Python's Flying Circus*, illustrates the way comedy often trades on the absurd:

the clash of images, words and concepts that give rise to absurdity can very often make us laugh. Deliberately concocted situations – a self-defence class to ward off assailants wielding fresh fruit, a steeplechase featuring a field of identical Queen Victorias, and so on – can be the stuff of comedy, but comedians also have a nose for the kind of absurdity mentioned above. Think of the stock question that serves as a lead-in to a stand-up comedian's riff: 'Did you ever notice ...?' Here the comedian is encouraging us to take a kind of detached or off-kilter view of something that we may have taken for granted, in order to see that it does not make the kind of sense we took it to mean, that its parts or pieces do not fit together in the way we might have assumed. The absurd can be funny, but it can be tragic as well. (Kierkegaard remarks in *Fear and Trembling* that 'the comic and the tragic converge on each other ... in absolute infinity'[68].) The sight of soldiers by the thousands being sent 'over the top' in the face of machine-gun and artillery fire can strike us as absurd, though there is nothing at all humorous about it.

A person, situation, event or utterance may be absurd insofar as there is a clash or contradiction at work. There is a kind of metric of the absurd, which depends upon how far apart the clashing elements are: 'The magnitude of the absurdity will be in direct ratio to the distance between the two terms of my comparison.'[69] Camus's interest lies in a kind of maximal absurdity, what we might call the Absurd. What I mean here is that the absurdity that might beset particular situations and events is only a local absurdity, something confined to that situation, whereas Camus is interested in a more global form of it. We may now begin to see the work those intimations or feelings of absurdity are doing for Camus. The sense of the 'stage set' collapsing is not about one particular episode or event, such that my performing just *this* task in *this* situation is absurd (e.g. making 500 copies of a report to be read by just two or three people) but that the whole of it no longer really makes sense. Once I see my life as a recurring drudgery of demands and obligations, I can no longer become absorbed in the previous naive way; once the 'denseness and strangeness' of the natural world is revealed to me, then my reverting to a winter wonderland perspective is really a kind of amnesia or false consciousness; once I am struck by the 'cruel mathematics' of human mortality, then it is a kind of bad faith to go back to pretending nobody 'knows'. Camus thus claims that 'a man who becomes conscious of the absurd is forever bound to it'[70]. But if there is no going back, then the real question for Camus is how, if at all, to go forward.

▶ The varieties of suicide

Recall the conditionals that served as our starting point for understanding the central problem posed by 'The Myth of Sisyphus', what Camus dubbed the problem of suicide. As far as Camus is concerned, the antecedent of these conditionals can be safely asserted. The 'lucid reason' whose exercise creates a radical rupture between mind and world thereby shows – or perhaps thereby makes – life to be absurd. Once realized, there is no denying or revising this realization, but if we also accept these conditional statements as they stand, then by simple reasoning it would follow that life is not worth living and so that suicide is legitimate. Camus clearly wants to resist that conclusion, as he rejects both actual suicide and what he calls 'philosophical suicide' as legitimate or appropriate responses to life's absurdity. Let us start with his rejection of the real thing before turning to the philosophical variety.

Camus acknowledges that there is something effective about real suicide in relation to the absurdity of life in the sense that it puts an end to that absurdity: 'In its way, suicide settles the absurd.'[71] Is it not then a solution to the problem? There are a number of peculiarities with thinking about suicide as a solution in this context. First, the whole problem of absurdity was intimated in part by the realization of mortality, of that 'cruel mathematics' dictating my inevitable demise. Each of us has in store a 'unique and dreadful future', but the question here is the motivation for 'rush[ing] toward it' by committing suicide. If life is absurd because of my inevitable demise, isn't the absurdity of life only heightened by my bringing that demise about as quickly as possible? Isn't that to mistake the problem for the solution? Even leaving this concern aside, there is a further peculiarity about suicide understood as a solution to the problem of life's absurdity. Recall Camus's observation that 'there is no experience of death'. Death is instead the end of experience, its annihilation as far as worldly existence goes. Suicide 'settles the absurd' only by extinguishing it along with all experience, but then the one who commits suicide feels no relief from a sense of life's absurdity precisely because he or she no longer feels anything. There is, so to speak, a kind of overkill involved in suicide: it removes the experience of the absurd by removing too much or by removing the wrong thing, namely, the possibility of experience.

In many ways, Camus is far more interested in a different kind of suicide altogether, one that he sees at work in 'existential philosophies' such as those of Kierkegaard and Jaspers. (Heidegger is not mentioned in this context and we have to remember that the essay was written in 1940, prior to Sartre's coming out as an existentialist; it is not clear that they fall within the purview of Camus's critique.) Common to these philosophies is what Camus finds to be a 'forced hope' in the face of life's absurdity. That is, the existential attitude sees in the recognition of life's absurdity an occasion for 'a leap' – really, a leap of faith – that lends to the realization of life's absurdity a kind of poignant celebration. To acknowledge life's absurdity is to be given the opportunity to make a courageous plunge toward some unknown redemption, a hidden meaning that will make it all make sense in the end. Kierkegaard's knight of faith acts 'by virtue of the absurd', without reason or justification for his or her actions, but we are supposed to see in that an increased nobility rather than a thundering non sequitur. The latter is precisely how Camus sees it, as nothing grounds or motivates the kind of faith being celebrated here. It is *philosophical* suicide in its renunciation or denial of reason. According to the existential attitude, 'reason is useless but there is something beyond reason'[72].

One cannot here ask for a reason to think there is some such something, since it has been conceded that reason is useless. But without a reason, we seem only to be heightening the absurdity of life rather than getting beyond it. Ungrounded hope – hope where there is no reason whatsoever to believe in what is hoped for – is itself absurd. Those recommending philosophical suicide are not so much responding to the absurd, let alone overcoming it, as merely accepting it. Since there is no reason to think there is anything beyond reason – some hidden solution to the enigma life poses – then the real challenge is one of knowing 'whether I can live with what I know and with that alone'[73]. Living in this way, which involves continuing to live, is not about accepting the absurd but instead defying it.

▶ Defiance: this Sisyphean life

I have neglected thus far to comment on the significance of the title of Camus's essay. My delay follows Camus, as he does not discuss his mythological hero until the very end of the essay, in a kind of coda to the work as a whole. **Sisyphus** is a figure in Greek mythology, a king who committed various crimes both against humans (murdering guests at his court) and the gods (betraying a secret kept by Zeus). As punishment, in the underworld Sisyphus is condemned to roll a large boulder up a hill, only to have it roll back down, whereupon he will begin pushing the rock up once more. The pointlessness of Sisyphus's endeavour is readily apparent: he accomplishes nothing lasting by his efforts, as the task is reset immediately upon its completion. What is important for Camus is that Sisyphus – or at least *his* Sisyphus – knows this. He is under no illusion that he is getting anywhere by his efforts. A Sisyphus who thought that one of these times the rock would stay atop the hill, who held out hope for that happening or who thought that what he was doing was somehow important, that it contained some kind of higher meaning, any version of Sisyphus along these lines would earn only Camus's contempt. So would a Sisyphus who whined or gave up, who sat dejectedly against his boulder rather than putting his shoulder to the task. Any such Sisyphus would surely be no absurd hero. (Equally unheroic, of course, would be an oblivious Sisyphus, who toiled mindlessly like an ant scurrying about its hill.) What makes Sisyphus an absurd hero is his embodying a kind of performative paradox: he gives his task everything he has, while harbouring no illusions about the futility of his endeavours. His 'whole being is exerted toward accomplishing nothing'[74]. This is a kind of paradox in that the two aspects of Sisyphus's attitude would appear to cancel each other out: knowing that something is pointless or futile is a reason – indeed, a conclusive reason – not to do that thing. The question, 'Why bother?' would appear to go unanswered in such cases, but the lack of an answer does not bother Sisyphus or at least does not diminish his efforts. Giving the task his all is the only way he can defy the gods, the only way he can show that 'he is superior to his fate. He is stronger than his rock.'[75] Camus goes so far as to say in closing that 'one must imagine Sisyphus happy'[76].

It is not difficult, I think, to discern Sisyphean patterns in our lives here, outside the underworld. A rather trivial one is embodied in the child's query as to why he or she needs to make the bed in the morning, since it will only get messed up again that very evening. Much of what we do has this kind of 'reset' feature: we eat only to get hungry again, sleep only to get tired once more, strive to raise our children well, so they can be the kind of parents who raise their children well, and so on. While there are satisfactions to be had in various accomplishments and moments of pleasure, no satisfaction lasts for long: we must set off in pursuit of some new goal or simply sit idly, zoned out (and what exactly is the point of *that*?). We are condemned either to strive or be bored: contentment – lasting contentment – is not an option. Such a realization can be the occasion for despair, but for Camus it serves only to intensify one's efforts without forgetting the futility of doing so. The absurd hero's revolt 'is the certainty of a crushing fate, without the resignation that ought to accompany it'[77]. Such revolt 'is what gives life its value. Spread out over the whole length of a life, it restores its majesty to that life.'[78] We can now see more clearly just how far Camus intends to take us from the kind of conditional statements with which we began. We started with the intuition that the worth of one's life depended crucially on its meaning: if one feels one's life has no meaning, then that life is not worth living. Camus goes further than simply denying the connection between these two ideas, such that the worth of one's life is independent of questions concerning its meaning. He goes further by asserting that its worth is *increased* by the absence of meaning: 'It was previously a question of finding out whether or not life had to have a meaning to be lived. It now becomes clear, on the contrary, that it will be lived all the better if it has no meaning.'[79]

This last assertion helps to explain why Camus thinks we must imagine Sisyphus happy: his task is patently pointless, but that only serves to intensify the kind of grim satisfaction he takes in his defiant stance. We can now see more explicitly the problems that beset identifying Camus with existentialism, namely, that Camus is all about – and only about – the celebration of **defiance**. At the same time, I cannot help thinking that Camus is perhaps cheating here. Seeing where he's cheating may, I suggest, allow him to skulk back into the existentialist fold (assuming he'd want to). Although Camus treats Sisyphus's predicament as a paradigm of absurdity, consider the following alternative: imagine that Sisyphus is again condemned to push a large boulder up a hill, only in this retelling, no matter how much effort he exerts, however much heaving, grunting, sweating and shoving, the boulder does not budge. Nothing – not an inch – and yet Sisyphus must continue to strain. And suppose further that this Sisyphus likewise knows the rock will never move, but keeps up the effort anyway. If the predicament of the standard version exemplifies absurdity, then this version surely does as well. But is this alternative Sisyphus still 'stronger than his rock' just because he sticks to it? Can we imagine this Sisyphus happy? Camus cheats in that he wrings from the Sisyphus story sufficiently vivid moments of satisfaction as to allow for a pride that is not simply perverse. These are the moments when Sisyphus, having pushed the rock to its summit, watches it roll and then makes his way back down. Sisyphus does manage to accomplish *something* – he gets the damn rock to the top of the hill over and over again – and so we might understand why he can muster a feeling of satisfaction. His fate, absurd though it is, is nonetheless structured by goals that he manages to reach. Take that away, and it is hard indeed to say that we *must* imagine Sisyphus happy.

What I am calling cheating on Camus's part starts much earlier in the essay than his recounting of the Sisyphus myth at its close. All of the sketches he offers of the 'absurd man' in Part II of the essay – Don Juan, the Actor, the Conqueror – are described as embodying a kind of striving despite the recognition of ultimate futility. Don Juan seduces only to make off to seduce once more; the Actor strives to fully inhabit a persona only to have the stage set collapse in a matter of hours; the Conqueror knows that anything gained in his struggle will only spur him to further action. Notice that in all of these cases, there is a great deal we can point to in terms of accomplishment and satisfaction, even if there is no ultimate goal we can specify. None of these characters is really a case where his 'whole being is exerted toward accomplishing nothing'. All of the absurd heroes Camus sketches strive for things that they – and we, for the most part – can recognize as worth pursuing, and so any kind of 'defiance' that might be involved does not seem particularly hard-won. I thus find it hard to take Camus at his word when he says that consciousness or lucidity is all that matters: 'Being aware of one's life, one's revolt, one's freedom, and to the maximum, is living, and to the maximum. Where lucidity dominates, the scale of values becomes useless.'[80] Quantity trumps quality, according to Camus, so that 'what counts is not the best living but the most living'[81]. I have tried to suggest, however, by my appeal to an alternative Sisyphus whose rock never moves, as well as to Camus's own choice of absurd heroes, that there is more in the way of value lurking in his views than he sometimes allows. His hero is not really a defiant celebrant of our life's absurdity, but someone in hot pursuit of what he or she cares most about.

7

De Beauvoir and the ambiguity of existence

... man must not attempt to dispel the ambiguity of his being, but ... accept the task of realizing it.

Simone de Beauvoir, The Ethics of Ambiguity

▶ Ambiguity versus absurdity

Although she was born five years before Camus, I depart from strict chronology to present de Beauvoir after him. I do so because her views can be more clearly delineated by seeing how they are opposed to those of Camus. As I noted at the outset of Chapter 6, in addressing the question of Camus's affiliation with existentialism, de Beauvoir asserts both the unoriginality of Camus's trope of absurdity and its distance from anything espoused by existentialism. Although Camus is not mentioned explicitly in her book *The Ethics of Ambiguity*, it is difficult while reading it not to think of Camus as playing the role of a kind of implicit sparring partner (if not, indeed, a punching bag) for long stretches of her discussion. This is especially tempting when, at several junctures, de Beauvoir juxtaposes explicitly her favoured notion of ambiguity with the notion of absurdity, which, as we have seen, is central to Camus's views.

In ordinary parlance, to characterize something as fraught with ambiguity suggests that the thing in question is in some way inexact, unclear, uncertain, indefinite or indeterminate. If someone says something ambiguous, it means that the words can be taken in more than one way (and without its being in any way clear which way is to be preferred). Gestures and actions may likewise be ambiguous: was he being flirty or only friendly? Was she expressing irritation or just fatigue? While these sorts of ambiguity may resolve themselves upon further investigation (I found out she was indeed only tired), that need not be the case: I might not myself be clear about whether I meant to be flirtatious or simply friendly. Ambiguity thus leaves something's meaning or significance open and it is this lack of determinacy or finality that de Beauvoir wishes to emphasize. And here we risk conflating her ideas with those of Camus: said in a slightly different tone of voice, with a slightly different inflection, the ideas animating the notion of ambiguity might well be (mis)understood as warranting the claim that human existence is indeed absurd. That meaning is not, and can never be, fixed is not the same as saying that meaning is lacking:

> *The notion of ambiguity must not be confused with that of absurdity. To declare that existence is absurd is to deny that it can ever be given a meaning; to say that it is ambiguous is to assert that its meaning is never fixed, that it must be constantly won.*[02]

Camus declares in that 'I don't know whether this world has a meaning that transcends it. But I know that I do not know that meaning and that it is impossible for me just now to know it.'[03] The unavailability of any such 'transcendent' meaning leads Camus to declare that human life is therefore absurd, but it is just such an inference that de Beauvoir wishes to block. No such conclusion follows from the absence of that kind of meaning. What it shows instead is that whatever meaning life – my life – is to have must be worked out in

▲ Simone de Beauvoir (1908–86).

the ongoing living of my life. As something to be worked out, it is not something fixed or settled, but open or at issue. Hence her idea of ambiguity. A fully human life is one led in the recognition or acknowledgement of the absence of a settled – let alone transcendent – meaning. 'Nothing is decided in advance, and it is because man has something to lose and because he can lose that he can also win.'[84] Camus, by contrast, accepts defeat from the start.

That Camus simply throws in the towel is evident in his assumption of the figure of Sisyphus as his hero. In doing so, he thereby levels down the patterns and possibilities of life to a series of futile and repetitive tasks on the model of Sisyphus's exerting himself over and over again to get his rock up the hill. De Beauvoir finds little that is heroic in such futile activity:

> In the face of an obstacle which it is impossible to overcome, stubbornness is stupid. If I persist in beating my fist against a stone wall, my freedom exhausts itself in this useless gesture without succeeding in giving itself a content. It debases itself in vain contingency.[85]

I noted in Chapter 6 that Camus cheats in his appeal to Sisyphus, since there is still some measure of success or triumph in his activity. A Sisyphus who continually pushed against an unmoving rock would be a better model of absurdity, but one where any hint of heroism would be lacking. Even so, the emptiness of Sisyphus's 'accomplishments' is painfully evident, which makes Camus's admiration all the more puzzling. As de Beauvoir remarks, 'there is no more obnoxious way to punish a man than to force him to perform acts which make no sense to him, as when one empties and fills the same ditch indefinitely, when one makes soldiers who are being punished march up and down, or when one forces a schoolboy to copy lines.'[86] The distinction between activities that are empty and futile and those that are worthwhile is one we draw *within* human life rather than determine from some outside perspective.

Camus's adoption of just such a perspective is what leads him to overlook the difference.

What Camus misses is the way 'a freedom can not will itself without willing itself as an indefinite movement'[87]. Activity undertaken within a field of open possibilities is altogether unlike the kind of empty repetition Camus sees at work in all human endeavour.

▶ Self and other

I have introduced de Beauvoir's conception of human existence as inherently ambiguous by contrasting it with Camus's notion of absurdity. While her divergence from Camus is certainly noteworthy, her proximity to Sartre is even more so. Both biographically and philosophically, de Beauvoir and Sartre are deeply intertwined with one another: de Beauvoir first met Sartre when she was only 21 years old while both were studying philosophy and they become nearly constant companions. Given their close affiliation during the years leading up to and encompassing the emergence of existentialism, it is difficult – if not impossible – to treat their philosophical views as entirely separate from one another. But this is not to say that de Beauvoir's contributions to existentialism simply duplicate those made by Sartre. There is indeed considerable convergence owing to the close collaboration between them, but there is divergence as well. I will try to emphasize those places where de Beauvoir can be understood as departing from Sartre and perhaps even correcting some of the more problematic aspects of his outlook. These departures are especially evident in her conception of the relation between *self* and *other* and in her treatment of the notion of a **situation**.

As I noted in Chapter 5, one of the most famous quotes associated with Sartre is the line from *No Exit*, 'Hell is other people.' But as I further noted at the conclusion of the chapter, much of what Sartre says in his later 'The Humanism of Existentialism' tempers the dark, hellish outlook he offered in earlier philosophical and dramatic works. Sartre came to recognize how an individual's realization of his or her freedom is not indifferent to the freedom of others: a being who affirms his or her own freedom can at the same time 'only want the freedom of others'. While Sartre seems to embrace belatedly, and almost reluctantly, a more reciprocal conception of freedom after the more agonistic account in *Being and Nothingness*, de Beauvoir in *The Ethics of Ambiguity* gives pride of place to precisely that kind of reciprocity. There she sets out to debunk thoroughly the image of the lone individual freely determining his fate irrespective of anyone else. Again with a veiled reference to Camus, who appeals to the 'conqueror' as one of his three paradigmatic 'absurd men', de Beauvoir singles out the 'adventurer' as the distorted image of the existentialist hero: '[If] existentialism were solipsistic, as is generally claimed, it would have to regard the adventurer as its perfect hero.'[88]

That the adventurer who sallies forth indifferent to others is anything but a perfect hero can be seen by recalling the difference between an adventure – something undertaken in the real world – and a mere game: 'What distinguishes the adventure from a simple game is that the adventurer does not limit himself to asserting his existence in solitary fashion. He asserts it in relationship to other existences. He has to declare himself.'[89] Even in the notion of adventure, there is thus the possibility of realizing the reciprocal dimensions of freedom. The adventurer 'can become conscious of the real requirements of his own freedom, which can will itself only by destining itself to an open future, by seeking to extend itself by means of the freedom of others'[90]. Such a man can rise above being a mere adventurer, in contrast to the more Camus-like hero: 'The man we call an adventurer, on the contrary, is one who remains indifferent to the content, that is, to the human meaning of his action, who thinks he can assert his own existence without taking into account that of others.'[91] What de Beauvoir refers to here as 'the human meaning of his action' underscores the ways in which meaning is not a purely private or solitary affair: the meaning or significance of my actions is not for me alone to judge. But the issue is not just about who is in the best position to judge the meaning of an action. Rather, it is about what makes up the meaning or significance of an action; here, others play an essential role, since that meaning is sensitive to, and so partly determined by, how it affects (and is perceived) by others. While I may be having the time of my life racing about in my sports car, swigging from cans of beer, what I am doing is reckless, harmful, insensitive etc. because of the ways others are at risk. My acting in that way impinges on their freedom. But de Beauvoir notes that 'to will oneself free is also to will others free. This will is not an abstract formula. It points out to each person concrete action to be achieved.'[92]

We can see in de Beauvoir's appeal to the reciprocal dimensions of freedom a significant point of contact with at least some of what Sartre says, especially in *Existentialism is a Humanism*. There, as we have seen, Sartre emphasizes the sense of responsibility that comes with human existence, where that extends from my own existence to 'all mankind'. The ways in which the freedom of others is at issue in my own choices and actions underscores this kind of responsibility. But we can also see de Beauvoir as correcting some errant steps Sartre takes in that same essay, for example when he approvingly cites the worry that animates Dostoyevsky's *The Brothers Karamozov*, namely, that 'If God does not exist, everything is permissible.' Sartre declares this to be 'the starting point of existentialism'[93]. As de Beauvoir sees it, it is just that lack of excuses that undercuts the idea that 'everything is permissible if God does not exist'. What Sartre does not see is the way his endorsement of Dostoyevsky cuts against his own broader ideas of freedom and responsibility. It is precisely because we – and we alone – are responsible for our existence that not everything is permissible. 'A God can pardon, efface, and compensate. But if God does not exist, man's faults are inexpiable.'[94]

▶ Resituating situations

Despite her divergence from Sartre, de Beauvoir's gloss on Dostoyevsky's pronouncement still gives pride of place to the notion of responsibility, much as Sartre does. As we saw in Chapter 5, Sartre's conception of responsibility is without limit or restriction: even events that seem to befall us from without, such as the outbreak of war, are nonetheless things that we in some sense choose. *The* war becomes *my* war when I choose to engage in it, rather than desert. I noted already that there was something forced about Sartre's picture of responsibility, since my choices are conditioned or shaped by factors beyond my control. Choices are conditioned or constrained by the situation in which they must be made, and just what situation I find myself in is not entirely up to me. Sartre does on occasion seem to recognize this, as when he rejects the 'immoralist' French writer Andre Gide's 'theory of the gratuitous act'. According to Sartre, 'Gide does not know what a situation is.'[95] The charge here appears to be that Gide does not recognize the way situations are 'complex social' phenomena, charged with a meaning or significance that does not determine my choice, but still delineates a range of choices I must either make or shirk (and in shirking, I still have chosen). Choosing not to participate in a war only makes sense when a war has broken out. I cannot make that choice one way or another when sitting idly at home in a time of peace.

So there are glimmers of recognition in Sartre of ways situations shape and condition choice and these help to mitigate some of Sartre's more extreme remarks about human freedom. But a glimmer is one thing; fully exploring the complexity of situations and their role in understanding responsibility is another. We can see much more of the latter in de Beauvoir. While Sartre may acknowledge that situations impose some constraint or shape on human freedom, he does not see how deep that imposition runs. What I mean here is that Sartre does not pay much attention – at least in his writings of the 1940s – to the way certain situations can be sufficiently oppressive so as not only to restrict the range of choices available to an individual but even to deform or efface his or her capacity for choice. In *The Ethics of Ambiguity*, de Beauvoir notes how 'there are beings whose life slips by in an infantile world because, having been kept in a state of servitude and ignorance, they have no means of breaking the ceiling which is stretched over their heads'[96]. She explains:

> *To the extent that they respected the world of the whites the situation of the black slave was exactly an infantile situation. This is also the situation of women in many civilizations; they can only submit to the laws, the gods, the customs, and the truths created by the males.*[97]

De Beauvoir's point here is that it would be wrong to condemn the slaves and women she describes for failing to take responsibility for their situation, for in some way failing to choose otherwise than as they did. The conditions here are such that there is simply no issue of choice. Such individuals 'have no instrument, be it in thought or by astonishment or anger, which permits them to attack the civilization which oppresses them'[98]. De Beauvoir does not say here how such people may come by the 'instrument' that does permit them to overcome their oppression, but once available, the oppressed have a responsibility to use it: 'But once there appears a possibility of liberation, it is resignation of freedom not to exploit the possibility, a resignation which implies dishonesty and which is a positive fault.'[99]

De Beauvoir's impersonal formulation in the last remark – 'once there appears a possibility of liberation' – indicates that the ways in which situations change shape do not depend in clearly delineated ways on individual choice. Indeed, once we recognize the complexity of the social conditions that generate oppression, individual choice can come to seem very anaemic. What I mean here is that if the 'possibility of liberation' depends on a reconfiguration of the broad social conditions in which people grow up and live out their lives, then it is difficult to see how that possibility might be realized solely through individual choice. Consider the case of women, which de Beauvoir explores at considerable length in her landmark work *The Second Sex*. If a woman has grown up in a society that actively inhibits the development of girls, then it is very likely, as the above passages attest, that she will come to identify herself in terms that reflect that inferior status. She, as much as men, will see herself as inferior, as the 'weaker' sex, and she may promote those inhibiting and oppressive structures when it comes to the next generation, i.e. she will raise her sons and daughters in ways that continue to encourage that identification. (As de Beauvoir drily notes, 'The fact is that men encounter more complicity in their woman companions than the oppressor usually finds in the oppressed.'[100]) But suppose an individual woman comes to view things otherwise, to see that her society is indeed oppressive to women and to see at the same time that she has the capacity to choose something other than, say, being a housewife or a mother. How, in that situation, does the one insightful woman exercise that capacity to choose? If the society is genuinely oppressive to women, as has largely been the case throughout human history, then very few, if any, genuine options or opportunities will be open to her. She will have open to her none of the choices available to men, and so in that way her capacity to choose will lie fallow. (There have been, of course, supremely talented women who have managed to overcome these conditions to excel in male-dominated fields, but such exceptional cases only reinforce how pervasive the rule of oppression is.) The wrong here 'comes from a situation in the face of which all individual behaviour is powerless'[101].

The idea here is that the individual woman cannot, just like that, choose to have a new range of choices available to her. Consider de Beauvoir's remarks on what awaits a young woman who simply ventures out alone, which some of the contemporary discussions of sexual assault, particularly on college campuses, echo to a dispiritingly strong degree: 'If she wanders absentmindedly, her thoughts elsewhere, if she lights a cigarette in a café, if she goes to the cinema alone, an unpleasant incident can quickly occur.'[102] While such a young woman has it within her power to choose to venture out alone, which itself is an advance over many more repressive societies, the extent to which such ventures are fraught with threats of danger and bodily harm is not really under her control. What is required is change on a larger scale, such that the whole shape of the situation changes in dramatic ways. These changes might include how children are raised and educated, so that boys and girls are not raised with different expectations and opportunities; how men view women, as partners and co-workers, for example, rather than subservient and submissive objects of sexual gratification or minders of the domestic hearth; how girls and women view themselves and one another, so as not to be complicit in the structures that have served to oppress them; how violence against women in both overt and more subtle forms is viewed and responded to; and so on. For de Beauvoir, a society that enacted these sorts of changes would be a society capable of 'restoring woman's singular sovereignty'[103]. This would be a society where women, just as much as men, are allowed and encouraged to an equal degree to become who they are.

Postscript

I began this discussion by citing Rabbi Zusya's 'Query of Queries'. I leave it to the reader as an exercise to determine in detail how that query fares in relation to the several existentialist views we have examined. It is by no means an easy task, in part because each view will bring to bear different considerations in spelling out what it means to be – and fail to be – an individual. I will note only that it is far easier in each case to say what failure looks like than to give an adequate account of success. Indeed, it may be that there is no success in the absolute sense. The stark character of Zusya's parable suggests that the query is inevitable, that the judgment which awaits us will always ask about our failings and shortcomings in the project of becoming who we are. The point of the parable might then be understood as encouraging us to attend to those shortcomings so as to diminish their number and severity, but without any promise that they will be reduced to zero. My sense is that existentialism is not far removed from this way of understanding Zusya's query. What is important is that the question arises and provokes its peculiar form of anxiety. In other words, what is important about the parable for existentialism is that it serves as a reminder that we are always *on the way* to becoming who we are, which means that we are beings who always have the sense that we can fail – and maybe are failing – at being who we are. The question grips us, even though, or maybe because, it is paradoxical. As a paradox, it does not admit of an easy response or solution. Indeed, as the existentialist sees it, any Zusya who confidently said 'But I just am Zusya' would be about the worst kind of failure there could be.

Key philosophical concepts

1 **Absurdity** is a function of the contradiction between two elements of a situation. For Camus, the foremost absurdity is the clash between humanity's desire for understanding and meaning and a world that is foreign to any such desire.

2 **Ambiguity** is de Beauvoir's term for the open-ended character of human existence. The meaning of human existence is not something that can ever be fully settled or determined.

3 **Anguish** is, for Sartre, an inescapable feature of human existence connected with the responsibility for one's own existence and, by extension, 'all mankind'.

4 **Anxiety** is Heidegger's term for a fundamental breakdown in human existence, wherein one experiences oneself as detached from the life and world in which one had been absorbed.

5 **Atheism** is the view that God does not exist. Atheism plays a prominent role in Sartre and de Beauvoir's conception of existentialism. While Camus never quite declares his atheism, he finds any appeal to God to be unacceptable to the 'absurd man', who relies only upon what he understands.

6 **Authenticity** is central to Heidegger's philosophy; to be authentic means to face up to being a being whose being is an issue for it and so can choose its possibilities.

7 **Bad faith** is Sartre's term for the lack of coordination between the two dimensions of human existence: facticity

and transcendence. Sartre refers to bad faith as an escape, in that someone in bad faith is not owning up fully to the complex character of human existence.

8   **Being-in-the-world** is Heidegger's term for the fact that human existence and self-understanding is always situated in terms of a meaningfully configured world. Heidegger's insistence on the primacy of being-in-the-world can be understood as a rejection of Descartes's idea of a self or soul whose essence is entirely separable from any worldly existence.

9   **Consciousness:** that we are conscious, self-aware beings is integral to existentialism, as it champions a lucid awareness of oneself and one's situation while condemning more passive and oblivious forms of existence. For Sartre, many of the key concepts associated with existentialism – freedom, anguish etc. – follow from the structure of consciousness.

10   **Dasein** is Heidegger's name for the kind of beings we are. Dasein is distinctive in that it is a being that has an understanding of being.

11   **Death:** the finite character of human existence. For Heidegger, awareness of death is part of what makes life meaningful; for Camus, awareness of death brings home life's absurdity.

12   **Defiance:** Camus's recommended response to the realization of life's absurdity. To be defiant is to press ahead wholeheartedly in one's projects while fully recognizing their futility.

13   **Despair:** a central concept in Kierkegaard's philosophy, which refers to a failure to be a self. Despair involves an imbalance between the two factors that make up human existence: freedom and necessity; the temporal and the eternal; the finite and the infinite.

14 **Eternal recurrence** is the idea that you will have to live your life in exactly the same way for all eternity. Nietzsche appeals to the idea as a way of measuring one's commitments to goals or purposes beyond this earthly life.

15 **Existence precedes essence** is, for Sartre, one way of describing the starting point of existentialism, which claims that there is no answer to the question of *what* I am (essence) prior to *how* I am (existence).

16 **Facticity** is the already-determined aspect of one's existence, which includes one's bodily make-up and the facts of one's past. Human existence always includes a sense of having-been.

17 **For-itself versus In-itself** is a key contrast in Sartre's philosophy. For-itself refers to the structures of consciousness as present to or for itself, while in-itself refers to things which just are as they are. Sartre argues that the principle of identity does not pertain to the for-itself, which is why conscious beings are beings for whom existence precedes essence. Human beings are an unstable combination of the in-itself (facticity) and for-itself (transcendence).

18 **Freedom:** a fundamental aspect of human existence as oriented toward the future as an open set of possibilities. As Sartre puts it, we are 'condemned' to be free in that we find ourselves as beings who have to choose who we are, but without having a choice about being that.

19 **God:** for Kierkegaard, faith in God is crucial to overcoming despair. Unlike for human beings, for God 'all things are possible'. Recognizing and accepting this is required for balancing the finite and infinite aspects of existence.

20 **God is dead** is Nietzsche's pronouncement regarding the modern age, where the idea of an absolute and external standard by which life might be measured is becoming less and less believable.

21 **Knight of faith** is Kierkegaard's name for the highest kind of individual. The knight of faith lives 'by virtue of the absurd' in that he lives fully committed to a project whose realization is beyond his power alone.

22 **Nihilation** is a key feature of Sartre's conception of human existence. Human existence is nihilating in that it is experienced as situated between a past it no longer is and a future it does not yet inhabit.

23 **Nihilism** is the felt loss or absence of any meaning or purpose to life and the world. Overcoming nihilism is a principal aim of Nietzsche's philosophy.

24 **Perspectivism** is Nietzsche's view that all views are perspectives, which means that they are always 'located', and so always in some way conditioned by that location and by the particularities of the one whose view it is.

25 **Resoluteness** is a key aspect of Heidegger's conception of authenticity. To be resolute is to choose one's own existence with a full awareness of its finitude.

26 **Sisyphus** is a mythical figure condemned in the underworld to roll a rock up a hill for all eternity. For Camus, Sisyphus represents both the absurdity of human life and its heroic defiance.

27 **Situation:** the meaningful context in which a subject finds itself and in relation to which he or she must choose. Human existence is always situated: there is no external or neutral position from which to choose who one is.

28 **Subjectivity** is for Sartre, the starting point of existentialism. The fact that human beings are self-aware beings implies that we are beings for whom existence precedes essence.

29 **Thrownness** is Heidegger's term for the way human existence is 'always already' situated in an ongoing world.

Thrownness refers to the way we find ourselves living lives we did not get to choose from the start.

30 Transcendence is the idea that we are future-directed beings. As Sartre puts it, a human being 'projects itself into a future, and is conscious of doing so'[104].

Key philosophical writings

This includes important philosophical writings beyond those cited in this work.

31 *Either/Or: A Fragment of Life* (1843) by Søren Kierkegaard; an examination of the different 'spheres of existence', which include the aesthetic, the ethical and the religious.

32 *The Concept of Anxiety* (1844) by Søren Kierkegaard; a foundational exploration of a key existentialist concept, with particular attention to the question of original sin.

33 *Philosophical Fragments* (1844) by Søren Kierkegaard; the work that the *Concluding Unscientific Postscript* (discussed in Chapter 2) continues.

34 *Thus Spoke Zarathustra* (1883–5) by Friedrich Nietzsche; a lyrical presentation of some of Nietzsche's key ideas, including eternal recurrence.

35 *The Antichrist* (1888) by Friedrich Nietzsche; a scathing critique of Christianity as an institution.

36 *Ecce Homo* (1888) by Friedrich Nietzsche; an autobiographical presentation of his philosophical point of view.

37 *The Twilight of the Idols* (1888) by Friedrich Nietzsche; a critical examination of the philosophical tradition, with particular attention to its inception with Socrates.

38 'History of the Concept of Time' (1925) by Martin Heidegger; a lecture course presented in summer 1925 that provides insight into how *Being and Time* took shape.

39 'The Word of Nietzsche: "God is Dead"' (1943) by Martin Heidegger; a later essay that reflects on Nietzsche's words as heralding the end of metaphysics.

40 'Letter on Humanism' (1947) by Martin Heidegger; his response to questions raised by the French philosopher Jean Beaufret concerning the proximity of his thinking to Sartre's lately announced humanistic existentialism.

41 *The Transcendence of the Ego* (1936) by Jean-Paul Sartre; an early work that critically examines standard conceptions of the ego or self and lays the groundwork for a more existentialist approach.

42 *The Emotions: Outline of a Theory* (1939) by Jean-Paul Sartre; an original analysis of the role of the emotions in consciousness.

43 *The Imaginary* (1940) by Jean-Paul Sartre; an examination of the structure of consciousness through reflection on the nature of mental images.

44 *The Rebel* (1950) by Albert Camus; a sequel of sorts to 'The Myth of Sisyphus' that considers the legitimacy of murder rather than suicide.

45 *Resistance, Rebellion, and Death: Essays* (1960) by Albert Camus; a collection of 23 essays reflecting on the problem of freedom.

46 'Pyrrhus and Cinéas' (1944) by Simone de Beauvoir; an early essay that rejects detachment in favour of engaged agency.

47 'What is Existentialism' (1947) by Simone de Beauvoir; a concise account of existentialism's core commitments.

Existentialist literature

48 *Notes from Underground* (1864) by Fyodor Dostoyevsky; an abject portrait of the solitary individual unable to engage meaningfully with those around him.

49 *The Brothers Karamazov* (1880) by Fyodor Dostoyevsky; a sprawling novel about three brothers and their father that considers fundamental questions concerning good and evil, fate and freedom.

50 'The Metamorphosis' (1912) by Franz Kafka; his most famous story, which concerns a travelling salesman who wakes one morning to find himself transformed into a giant insect.

51 *The Trial* (1925) by Franz Kafka; the ordeal of Joseph K, who stands accused of crimes whose nature is never explained.

52 *The Castle* (1926) by Franz Kafka; an unfinished novel about a land surveyor called only K, assigned to a village overlooked by a mysterious castle.

53 *Nausea* (1938) by Jean-Paul Sartre; his first novel, which centres on Antoine Roquentin, a young man who struggles with questions concerning meaning, freedom and action.

54 *The Stranger* (1942) by Albert Camus; a novel about Meursault, a young man unconcerned with any questions of meaning or value beyond his daily needs, whose fate hinges on a pointless murder.

55 *The Age of Reason* (1945) by Jean-Paul Sartre; the first novel in the 'Roads to Freedom' trilogy, depicting Mathieu, a philosophy professor forced to confront a situation that may compromise his cherished, although abstract, freedom

56 *The Reprieve* (1945) by Jean-Paul Sartre; the second part of the 'Roads to Freedom' trilogy set in Paris on the brink of war in 1938. Questions of freedom and action again figure centrally.

57 *The Plague* (1947) by Albert Camus: a novel whose hero, a doctor, copes with a plague that ravages a small town.

58 *Troubled Sleep* (1949) by Jean-Paul Sartre; the final part of the 'Roads to Freedom' trilogy that follows its characters as they adapt to life in occupied France.

59 *Molloy* (1951) by Samuel Beckett; the first novel in a trilogy, written in the form of an interior monologue.

60 *Malone Dies* (1951) by Samuel Beckett; the second novel in his trilogy, which recounts the ruminations of Malone as he lies dying.

61 *The Unnameable* (1953) by Samuel Beckett; the third and most abstract novel in his trilogy, which consists of the disjointed monologue of an unnamed character.

62 *The Mandarins* (1954) by Simone de Beauvoir; a fictionalized account of de Beauvoir's inner circle of philosophers and writers.

63 *The Fall* (1956) by Albert Camus; his last complete work of fiction, written in monologue, concerning the life and downfall of Clamence, a wealthy Parisian lawyer.

Existentialist drama

64 *Caligula* (published 1944) by Albert Camus; a play concerning the notorious Roman emperor, part of Camus's 'Cycle of the Absurd', which also includes *The Stranger* and 'The Myth of Sisyphus'.

65 *The Flies* (premiered 1943) by Jean-Paul Sartre; a play based on the Greek story of Electra and Orestes' quest to avenge the death of their father.

66 *No Exit* (premiered 1944) by Jean-Paul Sartre; two dead women and one dead man are locked in a room together for eternity. Nothing else is needed for their unending punishment.

67 *Waiting for Godot* (premiered 1953) by Samuel Beckett; his most famous play, in which two down-and-out characters pass the time while waiting for the enigmatic Godot.

68 *Endgame* (premiered 1957) by Samuel Beckett; a one-act play featuring four characters confined to a room surrounded by an unpopulated expanse.

69 *Krapp's Last Tape* (premiered 1958) by Samuel Beckett; a one-act play for one actor, in which Krapp marks his 69th birthday by reviewing recordings from throughout his life.

70 *The Condemned of Altona* (premiered 1959) by Jean-Paul Sartre; a five-act play about a German family in the aftermath of the Second World War.

Existentialism in film

71 *Ikiru* (1952), directed by Akira Kurowsawa; starring Takashi Shimura as a bureaucrat trying to find a meaning in his life after he discovers he has terminal cancer.

72 *The Burmese Harp* (1956), directed by Kon Ichikawa; starring Shoji Yasui as a Japanese soldier who fails to persuade his comrades to surrender in 1945 and becomes a Buddhist monk dedicated to burying his fallen countrymen.

73 *The Seventh Seal* (1957), directed by Ingmar Bergman; starring Max von Sidow as a man seeking answers about life, death and the existence of God as he plays chess against the Grim Reaper during the Black Death.

74 *À coup de souffle* (*Breathless*) (1960), directed by Jean-Luc Goddard; starring Jean-Paul Belmondo as a car thief who kills a policeman and tries to collect a debt and persuade a girl to escape to Italy with him.

75 *The Trial* (1962), directed by Orson Welles; based on Kafka's novel and starring Anthony Perkins as the office worker put on trial but never made aware of the charges against him.

76 *Winter Light* (1963), directed by Ingmar Bergman; starring Gunnar Björnstrand as a small-town priest struggling with his faith.

77 *Easy Rider* (1969), directed by Dennis Hopper; starring Peter Fonda and Dennis Hopper as two counter-culture bikers who travel from Los Angeles to New Orleans to discover America.

78 *Badlands* (1973), directed by Terrence Malick; starring Sissy Spacek and Martin Sheen as a young couple who go on a killing spree in the South Dakota badlands.

79 *Blue Velvet* (1986), directed by David Lynch; starring Kyle MacLachlan as a young man investigating a mystery related to a nightclub singer (Isabella Rossellini) and a group of criminals.

80 *The Sacrifice* (1986), directed by Andrei Tarkovsky; starring Erland Josephson as a man searching for a way to undo the outbreak of nuclear war.

81 *Groundhog Day* (1993), directed by Harold Ramis; starring Bill Murray as a weatherman who finds himself living the same day over and over again.

82 *The Thin Red Line* (1998), directed by Terrence Malick; based on an autobiographical novel about the battle for Guadalcanal in 1943 and its effect on a unit of men involved in the fighting.

83 *Fight Club* (1999), directed by David Fincher; starring Edward Norton and Brad Pitt as two young men who form an underground fighting club as a response to the deadening effects of everyday life.

84 *Being John Malkovich* (1999), directed by Spike Jonze; starring John Cusack and Cameron Diaz as a young couple who discover a portal that leads into the mind of the actor John Malkovich.

85 *American Beauty* (1999), directed by Sam Mendes; starring Kevin Spacey as a suburban father who has a midlife crisis after becoming infatuated with his daughter's best friend.

86 *No Country for Old Men* (2007), directed by Joel and Ethan Coen; starring Josh Brolin as a man who appropriates money from a drug deal gone wrong and is pursued by a killer (Javier Bardem) after the money, while a local sheriff (Tommy Lee Jones) investigates the trail of murders.

Existentialism and the fine arts

While existentialism is primarily a philosophical and literary movement, many of its central ideas find expression in paintings and other works of art.

87 *The Scream* by Edvard Munch: three of the four versions, two paint (1893, 1910) and two pastel (1893, 1895), are on show, at the National Gallery, Oslo, and the Munch Museum, Oslo, Norway.

88 *The Persistence of Memory* (1931) by Salvador Dalí: Museum of Modern Art, New York.

89 *Collective Invention* (1934) by René Magritte; Kunstsammlung Nordrhein-Westfalen, Düsseldorf, Germany.

90 *Guernica* (1937) by Pablo Picasso: Museo Reina Sofia, Madrid, Spain.

91 *Time Transfixed* (1938) by René Magritte: Art Institute of Chicago, Chicago, USA.

92 *Nighthawks* (1942) by Edward Hopper: Art Institute of Chicago, Chicago, USA.

93 *Hotel Bedroom* (1954 by Lucian Freud: Beaverbrook Art Gallery, Fredericton, Canada.

94 *Walking Man I* (1960) by Alberto Giacometti: Carnegie Museum of Art, Pittsburgh, USA.

95 *The 'Black Triptychs'* (1971–3) by Francis Bacon: the 1971 triptych is at the Foundation Beyeler, Basel, Switzerland, and the 1972 triptych is at the Tate Britain, London, UK; the 1973 triptych is privately owned.

Existentialist places to visit

96 Assistens Cemetery, Copenhagen, Denmark: the burial place of Kierkegaard (Section A); open to the public.

97 Nietzsche-Haus, Naumburg, Germany; the childhood home of Nietzsche; now a museum.

98 Nietzsche-Haus, Sils-Maria, Switzerland; the house where Nietzsche spent several summers in the 1880s; the library's extensive collections are open to researchers.

99 Die Hütte, Todtnauberg, Germany: the cabin in the Black Forest (still owned by his family) to which Heidegger retreated to ponder the question of being.

100 Les Deux Magots, Paris, France: the café, rendezvous of Paris' literary and intellectual elite from the 1880s, was frequented by de Beauvoir, Sartre and Camus.

Notes

1   Simone de Beauvoir, *The Ethics of Ambiguity*, trans. B. Frechtman (New York: Citadel Press, 2000), p. 34.

2   Søren Kierkegaard, *The Sickness Unto Death*, trans. A. Hannay (London: Penguin, 2004), p. 35.

3   Søren Kierkegaard, *Concluding Unscientific Postscript*, trans. D. F. Swenson and W. Lowrie (Princeton: Princeton University Press, 1974), p. 173.

4   Ibid. p. 75.

5   Ibid. p. 176.

6   Ibid. p. 173.

7   Ibid. p. 67.

8   Ibid. p. 116.

9   Ibid. p. 116.

10   Kierkegaard, *The Sickness Unto Death*, p. 43.

11   Ibid. p. 43.

12   Ibid. p. 45.

13   Ibid. p. 45.

14   Ibid. p. 44.

15   Kierkegaard, *Concluding Unscientific Postscript*, p. 182.

16   Kierkegaard, *Fear and Trembling*, trans. A. Hannay (Harmondsworth: Penguin, 1986), p. 72.

17   Ibid. p. 72.

18   Friedrich Nietzsche, *Beyond Good and Evil*, trans. R. J. Hollingdale (Harmondsworth: Penguin, 1990), aphorism (§) 22.

ALL THAT MATTERS: EXISTENTIALISM

19   Friedrich Nietzsche, *The Gay Science*, trans. W. Kaufmann (New York: Vintage, 1974), § 1.

20   Ibid. Preface, § 2.

21   Ibid. Preface, § 2.

22   Friedrich Nietzsche, *On the Genealogy of Morals*, trans. W. Kaufmann and R. J. Hollingdale (London: Vintage, 1989), III, § 27.

23   Friedrich Nietzsche, *Human, All Too Human*, trans. R. J. Hollingdale (Cambridge: Cambridge University Press, 1996), § 2.

24   Nietzsche, *The Gay Science*, § 108.

25   Ibid. § 58.

26   Friedrich Nietzsche, *The Will to Power*, trans. W. Kaufmann and R. J. Hollingdale (New York: Vintage, 1968), p. 9.

27   Nietzsche, *The Gay Science*, § 290.

28   Ibid. § 341.

29   Martin Heidegger, *Being and Time*, trans. J. Macquarrie and E. Robinson (New York: Harper & Row, 1962), p. 67.

30   Ibid. p. 96.

31   Ibid. p. 231.

32   Ibid. p. 230.

33   Jean-Paul Sartre, *Existentialism is a Humanism*, trans. C. Macomber (New Haven, CT: Yale University Press, 2007), p. 22.

34   Ibid. p. 20.

35   Ibid. p. 53.

36   Ibid. p. 29.

37   Jean-Paul Sartre, *Being and Nothingness*, trans. H. Barnes (New York: Washington Square Press, 1992), p. 707.

38   Ibid. p. 708.

39   Ibid. p. 708.

40   Sartre, *Existentialism is a Humanism*, p. 23.

41   Ibid. p. 27.

42   Ibid. p. 25.

43   Ibid. p. 24.

44   Ibid. p. 49.

45   Sartre, *Being and Nothingness*, p. 70.

46   Ibid. p. 110.

47   Ibid. p. 100.

48   Ibid. p. 100.

49   Ibid. p. 343.

50   Ibid. p. 343.

51   Sartre, *Existentialism is a Humanism*, p. 41.

52   Ibid. p. 49.

53   Ibid. p. 76.

54   Simone de Beauvoir, *Philosopical Writing*, ed. M. Simons (Urbana, ILL: University of Illinois Press, 2005), p. 209.

55   Albert Camus, *The Myth of Sisyphus and other essays*, trans. J. O'Brien (New York: Vintage, 1991), p. 3.

56   Ibid. p. 3.

57   Ibid. p. 3.

58   Ibid. p. 28.

59   Ibid. p. 12.

60   Ibid. p. 13.

61   Ibid. p. 14.

62   Ibid. p. 14.

63   Ibid. p. 14.

64   Ibid. p. 15.

65   Ibid. p. 15.

66   Ibid. p. 15.

67   Ibid. p. 15.

68   Kierkegaard, *Fear and Trembling*, p. 59.

69   Camus, *The Myth of Sisyphus and other essays*, p. 30.

70   Ibid. p. 31.

71   Ibid. p. 54.

72   Ibid. p. 35.

73   Ibid. p. 40.

74   Ibid. p. 120.

75   Ibid. p. 121.

76   Ibid. p. 123.

77   Ibid. p. 54.

78   Ibid. p. 55.

79   Ibid. p. 53.

80   Ibid. pp 62–3.

81   Ibid. p. 61.

82   De Beauvoir, *The Ethics of Ambiguity*, p. 129.

83   Camus, *The Myth of Sisyphus and other essays*, p. 51.

84   De Beauvoir, *The Ethics of Ambiguity*, p. 34.

85   Ibid. p. 28.

86   Ibid. pp 30–1.

87   Ibid. p. 31.

88   Ibid. p. 59.

89 Ibid. p. 60.

90 Ibid. p. 60.

91 Ibid. p. 61.

92 Ibid. p. 73.

93 Sartre, *Existentialism is a Humanism*, p.29

94 De Beauvoir, *The Ethics of Ambiguity*, p. 16.

95 Sartre, *Existentialism is a Humanism*, p. 45.

96 De Beauvoir, *The Ethics of Ambiguity*, p. 37

97 Ibid. p. 37.

98 Ibid. p. 38.

99 Ibid. p. 38.

100 Simone de Beauvoir, *The Second Sex*, trans. C. Borde and S. Malovany-Chevallier (London: Vintage, 2011), p. 757.

101 Ibid. p. 760.

102 Ibid. p. 749.

103 Ibid. p. 765.

104 Sartre, *Existentialism is a Humanism*, p. 23.

Suggested further reading

The following are works written with a non-specialist audience in mind.

Works on existentialism

Cooper, D., *Existentialism: A Reconstruction* (Oxford: Blackwell, 1999)

Crowell, S. (ed.), *The Cambridge Companion to Existentialism* (New York: Cambridge University Press, 2014)

Flynn, T., *Existentialism: A Very Short Introduction* (Oxford: Oxford University Press, 2006)

Guignon, C. (ed.), *The Existentialists: Critical Essays on Kierkegaard, Nietzsche, Heidegger, and Sartre* (Lanham, MD and Oxford: Rowman & Littlefield, 2013)

Joseph, F., Woodward, A. and Reynolds, J. (eds.), *The Continuum Companion to Existentialism* (London: Continuum, 2011)

Reynolds, J., *Understanding Existentialism* (Chesham: Acumen, 2006)

Wartenberg, T. E., *Existentialism: A Beginner's Guide* (Richmond: Oneworld, 2008)

Works on Kierkegaard

Carlisle, C., *Kierkegaard: A Guide for the Perplexed* (London: Bloomsbury Continuum, 2006)

Carlisle, C., *Kierkegaard's 'Fear and Trembling': A Reader's Guide* (London: Bloomsbury Continuum, 2010)

Hannay, A. and Marino, G. D. (eds.), *The Cambridge Companion to Kierkegaard* (Cambridge: Cambridge University Press, 1998)

Lippitt, J. and Pattison, G. (eds.), *The Oxford Handbook of Kierkegaard* (Oxford: Oxford University Press, 2013)

ALL THAT MATTERS: EXISTENTIALISM

Works on Nietzsche

Gemes, K. and Richardson, J. (eds.), *The Oxford Handbook of Nietzsche* (Oxford: Oxford University Press, 2013)

Magnus, B. and Higgins, K. (eds.), *The Cambridge Companion to Nietzsche* (Cambridge: Cambridge University Press, 1996)

Works on Heidegger

Blattner, W. D., *Heidegger's 'Being and Time': A Reader's Guide* (London: Bloomsbury Continuum, 2006)

Cerbone, D. R., *Heidegger: A Guide for the Perplexed* (London: Bloomsbury Continuum, 2008)

Dreyfus, H. and Wrathall, M. (eds.), *A Companion to Heidegger* (Oxford: Blackwell, 2007)

Guignon, C. (ed.), *The Cambridge Companion to Heidegger* (Cambridge: Cambridge University Press, 2006)

Mulhall, S., *The Routledge Philosophy Guidebook to Heidegger and 'Being and Time'* (London: Routledge, 1996)

Wrathall, M. (ed.), *The Cambridge Companion to Heidegger's 'Being and Time'* (Cambridge: Cambridge University Press, 2013)

Wrathall, M., *How to Read Heidegger* (New York: W. W. Norton, 2006)

Works on Sartre

Gardner, S., *Sartre's 'Being and Nothingness': A Reader's Guide* (London: Bloomsbury Continuum, 2009)

Howells, C. (ed.), *The Cambridge Companion to Sartre* (Cambridge: Cambridge University Press, 1992)

Works on Camus

Hughes, E. J. (ed.), *The Cambridge Companion to Camus* (Cambridge: Cambridge University Press, 2007)

Works on de Beauvoir

Card, C. (ed.), *The Cambridge Companion to Simone de Beauvoir* (Cambridge: Cambridge University Press, 2003)

Sandford, S., *How to Read Beauvoir* (New York: W. W. Norton, 2007)

Picture credits

The author and publisher would like to give their thanks for permission to use the following images:

Still from *Waiting for Godot* production © Rex/Donald Cooper

Kierkegaard portrait, based on a sketch by Niels Christian Kierkegaard (1806–82), Royal Library of Denmark

Kierkegaard family graves in Assistens Cemetery, from Thue/Wikimedia Commons

Nietzsche photograph by F. Hartmann (*c.*1875), scanned by Anton (2005)

Nietzsche's house in Sils-Maria © Manfred Glueck/Alamy

Martin Heidegger © Pictorial Press Ltd/Alamy

Jean-Paul Sartre © Rex/Roger-Viollet

Albert Camus © Mary Evans Library/Epic/AGIP

Simone de Beauvoir © Rex/Sipa Press

Index

ALL THAT MATTERS: EXISTENTIALISM

Also available in the series

Ziauddin Sardar

MUHAMMAD

BIOETHICS

Donna Dickenson

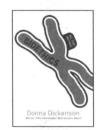

Julian Baggini

PHILOSOPHY

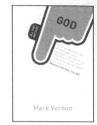

GOD

Mark Vernon

JUDAISM

Keith Kahn-Harris

LOVE

Mark Vernon

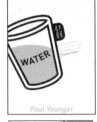

WATER

Paul Younger

Richard Huxtable

EUTHANASIA

Pascale F. Engelmajer

BUDDHISM

Andrew Silke

TERRORISM

HUMAN RIGHTS

Ivan Fiser

Johanna Oksala

POLITICAL PHILOSOPHY

Chris Goodall

SUSTAINABILITY

Alastair J.L. Blanshard

CLASSICAL WORLD

Mark Rowlands

ANIMAL RIGHTS

DEMOCRACY

Steven Beller

FEMINISM

Samantha Lyle
University of Warwick

HISTORY OF
MEDICINE

ALL THAT MATTERS

Tim Hall

SPACE
EXPLORATION

ALL THAT MATTERS

David Ashford

THE
ROMANS

ALL THAT MATTERS

John Manley

Barry Kemp

ANCIENT
EGYPT

ALL THAT MATTERS

MODERN
CHINA

ALL THAT MATTERS

Jonathan Clements

SHAKESPEARE'S
TRAGEDIES

ALL THAT MATTERS

Michael Scott

SHAKESPEARE'S
COMEDIES

ALL THAT MATTERS

Michael Scott

CYBER
CRIME
&
WARFARE

ALL THAT MATTERS

Peter Warren &
Michael Streeter

Ken Booth

INTERNATIONAL
RELATIONS

ALL THAT MATTERS

FUTURE

ALL THAT MATTERS

Ziauddin Sardar

THE RENAISSANCE

ALL THAT MATTERS

Michael Halvorson

Lorna Selfe

AUTISM
SPECTRUM
DISORDER

ALL THAT MATTERS

PLATO

ALL THAT MATTERS

Ieuan Williams

Camilla Ween

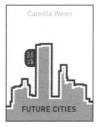

FUTURE CITIES

ALL THAT MATTERS

EMOTION

ALL THAT MATTERS

Sandi Mann

All That Matters books are written by the world's leading experts, to introduce the most exciting and relevant areas of an important topic to students and general readers.

From Bioethics to Muhammad and Philosophy to Sustainability, the All That Matters series covers the most controversial and engaging topics from science, philosophy, history, religion and other fields. The authors are world-class academics or top public intellectuals, on a mission to bring the most interesting and challenging areas of their subject to new readers.

Each book contains a unique '100 Ideas' section, giving inspiration to readers whose interest has been piqued and who want to explore the subject further. Find out more at:

www.allthatmattersbooks.com
Facebook/allthatmattersbooks
Twitter@_JMLearning